Angus  KU-679-508

BEES IN MY BONNET

ARROW BOOKS

Arrow Books Limited
17-21 Conway Street, London W1P 6JD

An imprint of the Hutchinson Publishing Group

London Melbourne Sydney Auckland
Johannesburg and agencies throughout
the world

First published by Hutchinson 1982
Arrow edition 1984

Printed and bound in Great Britain by
Anchor Brendon Limited, Tiptree, Essex

ISBN 0 09 934830 6

BEES IN MY BONNET

Suddenly we heard a heavy sound – a sound we were unable immediately and instinctively to identify and which caused us spasms of real terror. What terrible creature crouched behind the trembling rhododendron bushes, ready to spring at our throats?

Without warning a face appeared in the midst of the bush. A hawklike female face with a wide mouth – a mouth which suddenly uttered a heart-stopping screech. I had heard my father preach about the witch of Endor. Was this a witch of Southend, intent upon casting a spell on Neil and me, turning us perhaps into toadstools or even pillars of salt?

We lay there, desperately afraid but incapable of any physical action. And then the rhododendron branches parted and through them stepped Florrie Nail, cackling with laughter.

'I gi'ed ye a fricht, boys! I gi'ed ye a fricht!'

Also in Arrow by Angus MacVicar

Rocks in my Scotch

Fifty years ago my first book, *The Purple Rock*, was accepted for publication by Hutchinson (Stanley Paul). I dedicated it to my father and mother, the Rev. Angus John and Marjorie MacVicar. This one, the thirty-third of my books accepted by Hutchinson, I dedicate to their happy and inspiring memory.

Contents

1. The Ghost in the Graveyard

On 7 May 1912, I was three and a half years old. Archie, the eldest of my four brothers, was born that day. It is the first specific date I can remember; and I remember it for two reasons, both traumatic for a small boy in a big manse.

My father had been minister of the parish of Southend, at the Mull of Kintyre, for over two years. On an annual stipend of £180 he was yet able to afford two maids. One was Maimie, from Perthshire, five feet nothing of flashing temper and Gaelic kindliness. The other was Ina, a happy, red-haired girl from Campbeltown – the 'Wee Toun' – which embraces the loch of the song eight miles north of the Manse over a metalled road.

There is no question that in the Manse of St Blaan, with six bedrooms, a drawing-room and dining-room, a large kitchen and scullery and eight outhouses – one of them an earth closet – Maimie and Ina were kept busy all day, especially at times when my mother was bearing and nursing her babies, which occurred often during the first twenty-one years of her married life. Each time, on the whispered advice of her mother and grandmother, she prepared not only baby clothes but also a shroud for herself. The 'good old days' were anything but 'good', as far as women were concerned.

Maimie and Ina had to rise early, at about half past six, in order to set and light fires in the drawing-room and in the dining-room which served, too, as my father's study. And in the kitchen, where all the cooking was done on a great iron range. The fire in the range was also supposed to heat water in the copper boiler above it; but sometimes it didn't. Then Maimie, hitching up her black druggit skirt and white apron, would stand on one of the kitchen chairs (manufactured by

Sandy MacCullum, the local joiner), strike the pipes of the boiler hard blows with a poker and swear at them in the Gaelic. As a cooking medium, however, the range was efficient enough, though, along with the other fires, it devoured a ton of coal a week. (Before the First World War coal cost about ten shillings a ton. Your Scargills and McGaheys, where were they then?)

The fires had to be primed with paper and what Maimie called 'morning sticks', dry kindlers which she and Ina used to collect nearly every day from among the whins on the hillside behind the Manse. Then the porridge oatmeal, which had been steeping in water overnight, had to be salted and put on the range to cook – and be stirred regularly to avoid lumps – for the best part of two hours. No packets of instant Porage (*sic*) in those days. Ground from oats harvested in the fields around us, the meal came straight from the water mill at Machrimore, half a mile down the road. And savoury it was, eaten with a bowl of milk into which we dipped each horn spoonful.

For the minister, when he came downstairs at about half past nine, calling for his boots (polished in the kitchen the night before by either Maimie or Ina), there was supplied also a dish of ham and eggs: this to sustain his strength as he pedalled around the parish on his bicycle, visiting the old, the infirm and the recalcitrant. For the rest of us, porridge and a cup of tea were considered sufficient.

But on the morning of 7 May 1912, I became aware that something out of the ordinary was happening. Nobody wakened me in my small bedroom at the back of the house. I came downstairs, slowly and uneasily, and found nobody in the dining-room. The breakfast table wasn't even set. Suddenly frightened, I rushed to the kitchen. Ina was boiling kettles on the range. Maimie pushed past me as if I were invisible, carrying towels and jugs of hot water and muttering fiercely to herself.

'Where's Mamma? Where's Dadda?' I demanded.

Ina said, 'Your mother's not well. Your father's gone on his bicycle for the doctor.'

'I want to see Mamma.'

'No. Stay here. She'll be better soon. Here, sit at the table.' Her voice, usually so caressing, was hard, authoritative. 'I'll make you a piece.'

The world was turning upside down. I was no longer important. Nobody cared for me. Resentful tears had to be blinked away, because, even though I cried out loud, it seemed that nobody would listen.

I gulped down a jelly sandwich and went out into the garden: a huge garden with flowers and vegetables. There were gooseberries and currants and apple trees, too; but as their fruits were only in the early stages of growth I could not plunder and eat them to find comfort. Then I saw that Geordie, the odd-job man from the village, was already at work in the sunshine, earthing up potatoes.

Geordie had a ragged beard, though he was only middle-aged, and grey eyes that were cold and unfriendly. In his snarling voice he often used to call me names. For example: 'Get oot o' there, ye wee bugger!' When I told my mother about this and asked her the meaning of the word 'bugger' there was consternation in the Manse. If I used such a word again, I was told, my mouth would have to be washed out with soap and water. The reason for this was beyond my understanding. It was many years later that the exact meaning of 'bugger' was revealed to me, by an erudite schoolmaster.

Hatred for Geordie smouldered in my heart. That morning I saw him before he saw me. I took avoiding action by crawling along behind one of the rose beds and entering the outside closet, where gardening grapes, rakes and hoes stood beside the wooden seat. I pushed my pants down and clambered onto the seat. At that time small boys were just beginning to wear pants instead of effeminate frocks. The pair I wore had been designed and made by my mother from an old red dress of her own. A quarter of a century later she made ones for my son, Jock, on the same pattern and from much the same material. Dangling my legs and feeling low and unhappy, I suffered stoically the splintery feel of earth-encrusted wood on my bare bottom.

After a time I accomplished my duty. This made me feel

less martyred. Now nobody would threaten me with a tablespoon and the castor-oil bottle.

I used the torn-off corner of an old *Glasgow Herald* – a pile of newspapers served as a toilet roll – pulled up my pants and wandered off, by way of a broken down stone wall, into the hill where the whins grew. Whin spikes scratched my bare legs; the acrid, lusty scent of young summer in the whin blooms disturbed me. I felt unhappy again, even though a few young rabbits, scuttering on a bare patch of grass, afforded me temporary amusement.

I sat down on the bare patch, but even the rabbits were not prepared to be friendly. They took sidelong looks at me, then slipped off into the whins and disappeared.

By this time somebody ought to have discovered that I was missing and begun calling out for me. But no calls came, and I decided that the disappearing game was useless, as far as drawing attention to myself was concerned. I went back to the garden and moved round to the outhouses near the road, still keeping out of Geordie's sight.

In the stable I heard the sound of mewing. I pushed open the door. The interior was shadowed and smelt strongly of horse dung, because when people visited the Manse, or members of the congregation came to church on a Sunday in their 'machines', their horses were tethered here with bags of oats slung around their muzzles. I saw Susie, our ginger cat, crouching in a dark corner.

Surely here, at any rate, was a friend. I ran towards her, then stopped. Three small, damp, ugly kittens sprawled and squirmed beside her, and she was giving birth to yet another. It was the first time I had seen anything being born, and it made me feel scared.

But even in my ignorance I could see that Susie was discomfited. I knelt beside her and smoothed her fur, and she produced her last kitten and began to rub herself against my hand, purring. Soon, however, she withdrew her interest from me and began to lick her kittens.

I stayed with Susie and her family for a long time, marvelling at how quickly she transformed the palpitating, bedraggled blobs into the semblance of real kittens. I watched them nuzzle her stomach for milk. Eventually I forgot to be resentful and decided it was time to convey the exciting news of Susie's performance to everybody in the Manse.

I found Ina alone in the scullery, peeling potatoes.

'Susie's had kittens!' I told her.

She scarcely listened. '*Everybody's* having kittens this morning," she said. 'No!' She caught the sleeve of my jersey. 'Don't go through in there. Away you go outside again!'

This was insufferable. With deliberate intent I began to howl. I stamped one foot and would have attempted to circumvent Ina and run through the kitchen into the dining-room had not Maimie appeared in the doorway, no longer looking cross and harassed but with a dreamy smile on her face.

'It's a lovely boy,' she said to Ina. 'Everything's fine.' Then she caught my hand. 'Oh, *chiall*, they've been neglecting you, have they? Well, just you come with me and say hullo to your new wee brother.'

I became dumb. A brother? Nobody had prepared me for this. I felt lonelier and sadder than at any other time that morning. Even at this early stage the idea came to me that my best plan might be to run away. Then they would be sorry and come to look for me, and I would be important again. But a feeling of caution welled up. What if they *weren't* sorry and didn't come looking for me after all?

I followed Maimie upstairs. 'Your father and the doctor are in the dining-room having a refreshment,' she told me, adding with a chuckle, 'They need it, I'm thinking!' Why, I wondered?

My mother was propped up on pillows in the big bed. In a small cot beside it there lay an object which looked as ugly to me as the newborn kittens. I went to my mother, who looked paler than usual but very happy. She caught me to her and kissed me.

'Isn't he beautiful, Angus? He's going to be called Archibald. After my father, your grandfather in Appin. Being his big brother, you'll have to look after him and teach him how to be a good boy. I'll be depending on you.'

Well, this wasn't so bad. I was to be the boss, and Maimie was there to hear my mother say it. I looked down at the creature sleeping among the fleecy blankets, smelt the baby powder, resisted an impulse to do cruel things to the interloper and said, 'I'll look after him, Mamma.'

Having extracted this promise, my mother, like Susie, appeared to lose interest in me. She and Maimie began to croon over the baby. With sad dignity I retired and went downstairs to the dining-room where my father and the doctor were chatting together, tumblers in their hands. I smelt the aroma of what my father called 'spirits'. The golden liquid in the tumblers came from a bottle in the sideboard. I had been told that if ever I tried to drink from that bottle I should be poisoned and die in agony. Why did my father and the doctor not die in agony, too? If it came to that, why didn't Geordie get his mouth washed out with soap and water when he called me a 'wee bugger'?

My father patted my head. The doctor remarked that I was becoming a big boy.

'Susie's had kittens,' I told them.

I couldn't understand why they laughed. And I couldn't understand what my father meant when he said, 'We'll have to tell Geordie about her.' He added, 'Now off you go and play, Angus. It's a lovely day outside.'

No comfort here. Lacking desire to go outside and breathe the same air as Geordie, I trudged upstairs again and went to my bedroom, ignoring on the way the laughter and baby talk going on behind another door on the landing. I had a picture book detailing the adventures of a boy called Buster Brown. I climbed onto my bed, forgetting that my sandshoes were dirtied from the garden, and began to look through the book.

Soon, however, I tired of Buster Brown. I saw the earth from my shoes scattered on the yellow quilt. I got off the bed and, with difficulty, brushed the quilt with my hand. Some earth fell on the carpet. Eventually Maimie would chastise me for this, perhaps with a hard knuckle against my ear. But that was in the future. Just then I was so low in spirits that the prospect scarcely worried me at all.

I went to the window. Movement in the garden, beyond

the currant bushes and near the wall under the hill, attracted
my attention. Geordie was digging a hole.

He paused at last, stuck his spade into the turf and spat out
a stream of brown tobacco juice. He lifted a small bag from
the ground. From it he brought out a kitten. Holding the
kitten by the tail, he bashed its head against the wall and
threw it into the hole. He did the same with the other three.
Finally he filled in the hole and stamped down the earth on
top of it.

I was rigid with horror and hate. I wished I were a man.
Then I could have rushed out and struck him down with his
own spade. Even now I can feel the nausea of frustration.
Geordie was an ogre who deserved terrible punishment, but
I had no means of administering it.

After a while I went to the stable. Susie was moving about,
mewing. She came to me, rubbing against my legs. I took her
in my arms and sat down under the manger in one of the
stalls. It was dark and warm among the dung-scented straw.
Susie mewed and I cried, with anger and selfpity.

Maimie found us there. She took me inside and gave me
lunch in the kitchen and smacked me for not eating my
mashed potatoes and leaving most of the rhubarb tart. But I
didn't cry any more. Adults never changed their ways
because you cried.

In time I forgot about the kittens. I became more interested in Archie and did my best – which, admittedly,
sometimes fell short of perfection – to carry out my promise
to look after him.

He became the strongest and best-looking male member
of the family. At Glasgow University he graduated with
honours in English and won a soccer blue. He played cricket
right-handed and golf left-handed and showed no contempt
for those of us with less athletic skill.

During the Second World War he became an officer with
the 7/10th Argylls. He fought at Alamein and was wounded
there. In the action for which his commanding officer won
the Victoria Cross he was mentioned in dispatches.

In 1943 he fought in Sicily. During the battle for Catania in
July, the 7/10th Argylls were on the left of my battalion, the

2nd Royal Scots Fusiliers. When the immediate fighting was over I took a jeep and in some excitement bucketed across the scarred countryside to greet him. I was too late. The driver of an Argylls truck told me that my brother had been mortally wounded at Gerbini the day before.

I went to see his temporary grave. Then I returned to my battalion dug in on the low, damp banks of the Semeto. That night I lay in my bivouac shivering with a minor recurrence of malaria. I remembered the day Archie had been born. I had wept then because I imagined I hated him. Now I wept again, silently and secretly, because I knew that I loved him.

Being three and a half years younger, for a considerable time Archie remained a baby in my eyes and therefore unfit to join in proper adventures. My companion and mentor in such adventures was Neil MacLean, a son of the gamekeeper who lived up the road, in a rose-covered cottage by the burnside. He was my senior by about eighteen months, wiry and strong, with a sportsman's keen eye. Wielding his broomhandle bat left-handed, he could 'scud' the ball at rounders farther than anybody else in the infant school. I accorded him the respect his prowess warranted and followed him faithfully and sometimes fearfully on bird's nesting and bathing expeditions and into dangerous places in and around the Manse.

It was Neil who made me challenge the monster who lived in the larger of our two attic rooms.

My bedroom was a floor down from the attics, but the wall against which my bed was placed extended upwards past the ceiling into the wall behind which the monster lived. On silent nights, before going to sleep, I often heard him growling and clanking; and sometimes I imagined that the wall shook as he hurled himself against it.

For a long time I kept my fears to myself. I knew that if I revealed them to my parents – or to Maimie – they would look on me with disfavour and refuse to listen. (Even now, when the idea for a book occurs to me, I try not to discuss it with anybody before submitting it to a publisher. On the few occasions I have done so, the idea had always been devalued for me, all freshness and enthusiasm gone.) But at last one day during the Christmas holidays, I spoke to Neil about the monster.

He looked at me. 'Ye're daft!' he said.

We were in the stable, sitting in one of the mangers. 'I'm not daft!' I told him. 'Come on up. Maybe you'll hear him!'

We squatted on the bed in my room, eating hazelnuts found during a furtive exploration of the pantry downstairs. Neil and I had not yet been introduced to chewing gum. Our chewing of the nuts served the same nerve-calming purpose.

All was quiet, for a time. I made known to Neil my theory that the monster was a dry-land octopus.

'There's nae monster!' he said.

'There is so. I hear him often, moving and growling.'

He shook his head amused. But when there occurred a sudden clank and grumble above us, followed by what sounded like a long-drawn sigh, he was startled enough to swallow a mouthful of half-chewed nuts and jump off the bed.

I, too, slid to the floor. 'That's him,' I said, my voice a whisper.

We both wore short trousers, the cloth of which came from garments discarded by our parents. From one pocket Neil took a catapult fashioned from a Y-shaped hazel twig, elastic secretly removed from one of his sisters' knickers and a small square of leather (with a hole in the centre) cut from the tongue of an old boot. From another he took a handful of marbles, some jarries, some glessies. Jarries were dull, buff-coloured and lacking in liveliness, available in Mrs Galbraith's shop in the village at three for a penny. They were the kind with which, as a rule, poor marble players like myself had to operate, because the odd glessie we did happen to come by – multicoloured and expensive, costing a whole penny – was always won off us by the experts like Neil.

'Come on,' he said. 'We'll see what that is.'

'No. I'm scared.'

'There's nae monster in a manse. God wouldna allow it.'

The thought was comforting. 'What is it, then?'

'We'll find oot.' He was brave, compared with me a hero.
'Face up tae it!' he said.

Was it the first time I ever faced up to anything? The
exercise was hard then; it remains hard now, more than sixty
years later. Sometimes I slither out of it, by means of
self-administered doubletalk. But the result is always dis-
content, a condition even less supportable than moral or
physical fear. The awkward human factor called conscience –
unknown in the world of animals, however wise they may
seem – must surely come into it somewhere. And that day,
along with Neil, I discovered that 'facing up to it' can bring a
spiritual reward which is entirely human.

We emerged from my bedroom and began to climb the
attic stairs. On this winter afternoon they were unlit and
dark-shadowed. Neil went first, his catapult at the ready,
charged with a glessie. I followed close, in case I might
become detached from him and have to face the shadows
alone. We heard Maimie running water in the sink in the
scullery. Soon afterwards the monster above us clanked and
gurgled.

'Ach, I ken what it is!' shouted Neil, a burden lifted from
his tone. He put his catapult and its ammunition back in his
pocket.

His confidence fed mine. Quickly we climbed to the attic
landing and went into the room on the left. I was no longer
behind him. Bravely I had taken up position shoulder to
shoulder.

The sounds were coming from a small grey door in the wall
of the attic. Neil pushed it open, and there, in the darkness,
stood my monster; the main watertank, with tentacles of
dust-covered copper pipes jointed in bulbous lead. It was
bubbling and groaning as water flowed down the ancient
plumbing to the kitchen and scullery.

We laughed in wild relief. My own courage astonished me.
I climbed on to the tank top and with light-hearted
enthusiasm began to pull and push a metal lever. A ritual
slaying of the monster in my mind?

One clanking pull dislodged part of the tank top and
brought into view an enormous, dripping copper ball. Water

swirled and leaped and began to splash everywhere. With a yelp of fear I jumped away and scrambled out into the attic. Neil tried to thrust the copper ball back into the tank. He failed and followed me out. Water pursued us. We ran for our lives, downstairs, passing Maimie on the landing, demanding to know what was going on.

'The tank's burst!' shouted Neil, without pausing in his flight.

'There's a flood!' I contributed, not pausing either.

'*Chiall beannachd mi!*' screeched Maimie. 'Get Geordie! Get Geordie!'

Geordie was in the old barn, splitting logs with iron wedges and a heavy mell.

'You tell him!' I entreated Neil. My hatred for Geordie was constant.

He put his head round the barn door. He shouted, 'The tank in the attic's burst, Geordie!' Then he turned and we ran fast from the yard on to the cart track leading down to the burnside.

The afternoon was darkening. We crawled into damp whin bushes above the water. A smell of raw earth came from a landslide scar beneath the whins. Wild geese flew over, honking. In Kilblaan farmyard, half a mile away across the river, a dog was barking. Probably chasing hens for sport, Neil thought.

We had some nuts left. Cracking them open with our teeth, we chewed without pleasure. Our thin jerseys were poor protection against the cold.

The truth came to me that sooner or later, if I were to escape death by exposure, I should have to return to the Manse and face the consequences of our visit to the attic. Neil was luckier. He could go home and, by keeping quiet, escape retribution.

Imagination leaped higher and a terrible picture occurred to me of great waves of water pouring down from the attic, flooding the Manse and engulfing my parents, Archie and baby Willie – and Maimie. What if even now they all lay drowned in dark corners? The thought that Geordie, heedless of our warning and continuing to work in the barn, might have escaped only increased the misery which overwhelmed me.

As imagination continued to coruscate, I saw myself left alone in the world, perhaps at the mercy of Geordie. Panic seized me. I rushed out of the whins, leaving Neil gaping after me, and ran, panting, up and along the cart track to the Manse.

It was still there, in the dusk. Lights shone in the kitchen and dining-room and an upstairs bedroom. There was no water to be seen. Geordie had left the barn. I ran in by the back door.

In the kitchen the range was glowing. A paraffin lamp with a spherical glass oil-holder and a tall white globe spread a soft light from the dresser. Behind it, on the wall, a row of pewter ashet covers (hung in order of size) reflected its gleam. Maimie, now in sole charge because Ina had left to be married, was having a cup of tea at the wooden table, like the dresser another of Sandy MacCallum's products. She wasn't smiling.

'Where,' she demanded, 'have you been?' Adding, sinisterly, 'Your father's back from visiting. He wants to see you in the dining-room?'

'Was there a – a big flood?' I asked.

'If it hadn't been for Geordie there might have been. You're a bad boy, Angus! And now you're going to catch it!'

Inside me relief mingled with apprehension. Physically I was getting warmer and more comfortable. The Manse, my home, was normal again, without threat of flooding. But I had to face my father, who, in spite of being a minister of the gospel, was inclined to be hard hearted when dealing with the guilty.

The dining-room cum study was lit by a squat brass paraffin lamp on the oak table. The fire was bright, fed by some logs split by Geordie. They gave out an astringent smell, like the smell in Sandy MacCallum's joiner shop. Surrounding my father's rolltop desk in the corner by the window were laden bookcases. He himself sat in a big armchair, smoking a pipe. A spitoon lay within the hearth. My mother's chair, on the opposite side of the hearth, was empty. I imagined I heard

her upstairs, playing with Archie and the baby. I was alone
with justice. But that day I had faced a monster and
overcome it. Facing an angry father was now, surprisingly,
less fearsome than it had been before.

'Where's Neil?'

'He's – he's gone home.'

'I'll speak to his father tomorrow. Which of you damaged
the cock-ball?' Having known no English until he was five
years old, my father was always liable to think in the Gaelic
idiom, often, as he said himself, 'putting the horse before the
cart'!

Though tempted I did not fall. 'I did. But – '

'No "buts"! You might have caused terrible damage. I was
out. Lucky Geordie was here to put it right.'

Even had my father been in, it would have been Geordie –
or perhaps my mother, who was practical and pragmatic both
in deed and thought – who would have done the repair. For
the son of a crofter in North Uist my father was strangely
inept with his hands, except when wielding a garden spade. I
said nothing.

'Why did you do it?'

I couldn't explain about the monster and the euphoria that
had seized me when it had been laid low. I continued to say
nothing.

'All right. Bend over.'

I bent over the arm of my mother's chair. He got up and
smacked me twice on the bottom with his hard hand. At
other times, for sins less heinous in my opinion, he had taken
me to the piano stool in the drawing-room and used the back
of a hair brush.

'Never go near that tank again!' he commanded, clearing
his throat and spitting rather shakily into the spitoon.

I felt like crying, not because of a physical pain or fear but
because of the apparent lack of love for me shown by my
father. Here in the quiet parish on the tip of Kintyre, where
most people depended for news of the world outside on
secondhand copies of the *Glasgow Herald*, I was only
vaguely aware that a violent war was going on. That winter
afternoon in 1915 I had no idea that in a few months' time

my father was due to leave us for service abroad as an army chaplain. At the age of six I had no idea that he was sad and sick at the thought of going away, and that to punish me at such a time, in order to preserve the sense of discipline that would stand me in good stead when I finally sloughed off parental care, had cost him far more in unhappiness than it had cost me. It was years later, when my son Jock was growing up, that I understood.

My father was abroad with the Lovat Scouts, mainly in Salonika, for a year. When he returned we called him the Padre. Like everybody else in Southend, we continued to call him the Padre until he died in 1970 at the age of ninety-two.

Assisted by Maimie and supported by kind neighbours, my mother looked after the three of us during his absence. I tried hard to perform my duties as senior male member of the household but seldom felt that I achieved success. For example, I would willingly have helped in the garden, but Geordie was still there and I still hated being near him. When Peter Galbraith's stirks forced a way through the garden fence and plunged with cloven hooves across the soft front lawn, I was only too happy to try and chase them out, yelling and throwing stones with sweating vigour. But the extent of my inadequacy soon became clear when one of them got stuck in the bottom fence, a leg caught between crossed wires, and appeared about to injure itself in desperate struggles to break free. I became so agitated that I rushed away and hid in the attics, allowing my mother to go by herself to the farm and bring back Peter with a wire cutter. From an attic window I saw her running, hobble skirt pulled high to her knees, and felt shame that I remember to this day.

Part of my trouble has always been that I'm afraid of being afraid. (This may be one reason why my golf handicap has never been less than 5 and why now, in my advancing years, with a handicap of 12, I am sometimes afflicted by the 'yips' on the putting green.) My imagination was – and still is – particularly fertile, leading me to discover fear in situations which Neil MacLean, for example, would approach with cool common sense. I related ordinary life to high drama and, even now, often fail to realize that on the whole life is singularly undramatic. This may have helped me as a writer but is a considerable burden in a world in which chartered accountants rather than Robin Hoods wield the power and the glory.

While my father was away I would often wander off with the other boys on a summer evening to play on the beach at Dunaverty, essaying leaps from high dunes to the sand below and bathing in the sea, 'bare scuddy', when we became tired and hot.

Real excitement would attend the bathes if, as often happened, sinister grey warships came speeding through Sanda Sound, the two-miles-wide channel between the island and the mainland of Southend, whipping huge bow waves in against the shore and smothering us enjoyably with solid water and flying spray.

After the war it was the great ships of the Anchor Line that came ploughing proudly through the Sound – the *Caledonia*, the *Circassia*, the *Britannia* – bound for America with passengers and cargo. Today the Board of Trade has banned the sound as a passage for the big ships, and, in any case, all the lovely liners have gone, rendered obsolete by blind and stuffy aircraft. From my present home, overlooking Dunaverty Bay, the only passing vessels to be seen are fishing skiffs, whisky puffers from Islay, and oil-exploration craft, all waddling through the sound like ducks, and in the distance, far out in the North Channel, long and ugly container ships apparently chopped off fore and aft by giant hatchets. When we were boys, there on the beach, we could see, beyond the ships, the blue, round hills of Antrim, seventeen miles away across the narrow sea. For us they were hills of magic and romance as we imagined leprechauns in their shadowed valleys. Now the magic has gone, buried in harsh reports of bombs and bullets.

Sometimes, after one of those expeditions to the shore, darkness would have gathered before I reached home, and my mother would chide me for being late. I had no wish to make her feel anxious; but the fun was so good that a knowledge of time deserted me. She accepted my excuses more readily than my father would have done.

One evening, at dusk, pulling on my shorts and jersey after a bathe, I looked up and saw a light in the graveyard at Keil, half a mile along the shore.

'Do you see it?' I said to Neil.

'Ay. That's funny!'

One of the boys – Jamie the Clinker – said, 'My faither says there's a ghost at Keil.'

Neil glowered. 'Whit kind o' ghost?'

'An auld tinker. They thocht he was deid, but he wasna. They buried him alive. He comes up tae haunt them.'

I had an idea – only a vague idea, it must be confessed – that this story lacked the ring of logic. 'How does anybody know they buried him alive? They didn't dig him up again, did they?'

'They ken because his ghost comes up. That light. That's him, standin' at the door o' the auld chapel, lookin' oot tae sea. So my faither says.'

Neil must have seen that I was shaken. He put an arm about my shoulders. 'Ach,' he said to Jamie, 'yer faither's only tellin' yarns. Tae frighten ye indoors when it gets dark.'

That sounded good sense and made me feel better. Many a time Maimie had called me out of the dark at the Manse with the threat: 'If you don't come in soon the *bochcans* will get you!' (*Bochcan* is the Gaelic for a spiteful gnome.)

'Come on,' said Neil, the man of action. 'We'll hae a look.' And, as I hesitated, 'Ye're a meenister's son. There's only wan ghost ye should believe in – the Holy Ghost!' He screeched with laughter at his own joke, and I joined in, without conviction.

The moon was already riding high above the sea peak of Ailsa Craig to the south-east. I wanted to go home. I was afraid of the ghost. I was also afraid that I was going to hurt my mother by staying out so late. But Neil's philosophy was always to 'face up to things'. It had resulted in making a mockery of my monster. Perhaps it would make a mockery of this ghost, too.

We kept close together as we approached the graveyard

along the narrow, metalled road. In those days, when only two motorcars existed in the parish and horse-drawn 'machines' were seldom used at night, everything was quiet except for the occasional complaint of a seagull. In the salt-laden air midges moved in small clouds. We scratched continuously, which may have helped to take our minds off that light. It grew more brilliant as we came closer.

In the moonlight we could make out, inside the graveyard, the ruined walls of St Columba's chapel and the arched doorway beside which the ghòst was standing. Behind the graveyard were St Columba's footprints carved in a rock. Not far from the jagged north wall of the chapel was St Columba's Well, with whose water my father baptised the parish babies. I wondered if the ghost might not be that of a tinker at all but of a long-dead monk, perhaps even the great Columba himself. (Even then I knew a little about Columba, who came with his disciples from Ireland in the sixth century to bring Christianity to his kinsfolk, the Scotti. He was a hard man with sinners, according to my father, but with the needy and the poor in spirit kind and gentle. If only he knew how poor in spirit I felt at that moment.)

Suddenly the terror was on us. Two figures, looking huge in the dark, came leaping down from the wall by the graveyard gate. I yelled and tried to run, but Neil held on to my arm. 'It's only Big Doser and Kleek!'

I remembered having seen them on the beach, bathing some distance away from us, hulking lads of seventeen who worked as farm labourers. We always tried to give them a wide berth because of their reputation as bullies. No doubt they had noticed us making for the graveyard, guessed our purpose and hurried to be there before us, intent upon giving us a real fright. As far as I was concerned they had succeeded; but Neil and some of the others were hardier.

We outnumbered Big Doser and Kleek by four to one. 'Get at them, boys!' shouted Neil.

Our enemies were surprised. Small boys swarmed at them like bees, kicking and tripping and lashing out with fists. Presently both were down, scrabbling in the gateway, with Neil and his allies on top of them. I took my turn at striking and kicking, now that Big Doser and Kleek appeared to be helpless.

But triumph, as is the way of triumph, lasted only a few seconds. The enemy heaved themselves up, like twin Gullivers in Lilliput. We were thrown aside and came face to face with serious trouble. Big Doser's broken teeth showed in a grin of anger. His raw hands, protruding on wrist stalks from short, ragged sleeves, were curling, I imagined, towards my throat. Smaller and ratlike, Kleek was wiping blood and 'snotters' from his nose and howling intimations of vengeance.

Neil and the others ran. So did I. It was something I could do well. (I still can. Running, that is, in both its literal and metaphorical senses.) Big Doser and Kleek had no chance of overtaking us in the dark.

It was my mother, when I explained my lateness in dramatic and almost truthful fashion, who laid for me the ghost in the graveyard. The following night she took me for a walk and showed me how the moonlight fell on the granite of a polished and shining gravestone, embedded in the ancient wall of the chapel. Part of the inscription on the stone is as follows: 'Sacred to the memory of William MacMillan, died 17 October 1892, and of his wife, Margaret MacKerral, died 18 January 1892.' Years later it dawned on me that the Margaret MacKerral remembered on the ghost stone was a grand-aunt of the girl I was eventually to marry.

In a way, however, I had lost interest in the ghost. A psychic fear was supplanted by a physical one. Every time I visited the village or the shore I kept a sharp lookout for Big Doser and Kleek. But this fear was an exhilarating fear, almost enjoyable. If the worst came to the worst I knew I could outrun them both, like a gazelle which cocks a snook at lumbering rhinos.

2. Mull of Kintyre

The parish of Southend includes the Mull of Kintyre.

The Mull became famous 1800 years ago when Ptolemy, the Greek, made a map of it and named it *Epidion Akron*, 'the promontory of the horse people'. It became famous over a millenium later when Robert the Bruce took refuge with the MacDonalds in Dunaverty Castle before crossing the narrow sea to Rathlin and having his legendary encounter with a spider. It became famous yet again only a few years ago when Paul McCartney wrote 'Mull of Kintyre', the song which remained top of the pops for many week and provided newspaper men with a topical and romantic point of reference. All murders, shipwrecks and aircraft accidents occurring within fifty miles of Southend, on land or sea, are now described as having taken place on or near the Mull of Kintyre. Even the location of Paul McCartney's publicity pictures was not the actual Mull but a lonely shore at Saddell, some twenty-five miles to the north.

Paul McCartney was wise not to photograph or film the real Mull, which, if Kintyre is imagined as a giant leg, comprises only the big toe of the club foot. An enormous pile of metamorphic and volcanic rock spewed up in a series of ancient eruptions, its cruel magnificence, rising to 1404 feet at the summit of Beinn na Lice, has nothing in common with the sentimental softness of the song, which is derived from music and poetry first composed by Gaels in the sad flatness of the Hebrides.

McCartney's was not the first piece of music to be called 'Mull of Kintyre'. Some years ago a pipe tune was composed by Archie Duncan, one-time pipe corporal in the Royal Scots Fusiliers, to which he gave this name. It is well known in piping circles and has been performed on radio.

Archie still lives in Campbeltown, struck down with a rheumatic ailment caused in part by an experience in the Second World War during which he spent many hours in a lifebelt, floating helplessly in the cold sea off the Dutch coast, after the vessel in which he had been travelling was sunk by enemy gunfire. He now has four artificial joints, in his hips and in his knees.

He does not begrudge McCartney his commercial success. He is an artist, as clever at drawing and painting pictures as he is at composing tunes, and, like a true artist, derives his rewards – and his satisfaction – from the tributes he receives from all those who have enjoyed his work. Money means nothing to him. Appreciation does. As a writer myself – and, incidentally, a wartime Fusilier – I can understand this only too well.

Here in Kintyre we believe that long after the pop tune has been forgotten, Archie's pipe tune will live on.

The cliffs at the Mull, some over 500 feet high, and the boulders strewn along the tide lines below, like debris from a giant's quarry, make dubious appeal to gently nurtured visitors. Those with weak hearts or a tendency to vertigo are warned that even the road lassooing down to the lighthouse from the high moor can be a killer. And if a southerly or westerly gale is blowing, and they venture near the cliffs, they are advised to do so on hands and knees through the sopping peat hags. But at the end of this uncomfortable approach they will be rewarded – or perhaps intimidated – by a scene of splendour equalled only in parts of Sutherland, where, for example, Eas-Coul-Aulin, by far the highest waterfall in Britain and the fourteenth highest in the world, hurtles down 658 feet of sheer mountainside.

From the Mull, as the seaspray flies upward, salting lips and cheeks, there occurs, far below, the meeting of seven tides – from the Firth of Clyde to the east, from the Irish Sea to the south, from the Atlantic and the Antrim coast to the west and from the Minches to the north – a white-fringed maelstrom threatening to engulf any small craft which dares to challenge it. Out and beyond the tumult of the tides, in the near distance, lie the island of Rathlin, a lumpy boomerang, and, behind Rathlin, the beetling eminence of Fair Head and the lower lands of Ballycastle.

The eleven-miles-wide restless flow of water between the Mull and Northern Ireland is called the North Channel. During the two world wars convoys moved slowly through it, heading out into danger. In the First World War, as I remember, such convoys were escorted by cruisers and airships; in the Second World War they were festooned with anti-aircraft balloons and shepherded by darting frigates and destroyers.

Once, in the First World War, at about the age of nine, I was horribly scared by the sight of an airship, trailing some kind of rope or wire cable, as it appeared around the corner of a plantation near the Manse, heading, as I know now, for the North Channel. I was alone, searching for birds' nests on the low road to Kilblaan. It came straight for me, engines growling. I stood, shivering with fear, while it floated over, the dangling cable cutting a swathe in a nearby corn-field and snapping at least one roadside telegraph wire. As it receded in the direction of the Mull, I recovered mobility and ran, panting, to the Manse. I was gratified when my mother and Maimie came quickly outside to catch a glimpse of the disappearing monster. Having successfully given them the impression that on the Kilblaan road I had faced it alone, motionless and unafraid, I was even more gratified when Maimie remarked that I was a lot braver than she would have been. I began to persuade myself that though my father was away, in Salonika, as his stand-in at home I was playing a hero's part.

Seventy years ago, children in Southend seldom ventured to explore the Mull. The lighthouse was six miles from the village and seven from the Manse. The narrow road, though roughly metalled, climbed and swooped in hair-raising violence, making it a difficult one even for animals. In any case, parents were aware of menace in the high cliffs and promised their offspring painful punishment if ever they went near them.

I went to the Mull once, during the First World War, along

with my mother and some other youthful members of the Woman's Guild. We were taken to the high moor above the lighthouse – to Barney's Moss, a flattish green island in a rock-infested, turbulent sea of heather – in a farm cart drawn by a plodding Clydesdale mare. A farmer's daughter sat high on the front end of the cart driving, a man's cap on her head, a man's tweed jacket about her shoulders, her long, voluminous skirt tucked in close about her ankles. The rest of us crouched in the well of the cart, sheltering as best we might from a snell wind, though at one stage my mother moved forward and took the reins for a spell, reminding the driver that she, too, was a farmer's daughter. I remember feeling smugly proud of her.

The journey from the village took about two hours, because on long, steep ascents we had to lighten the horse's burden by getting out and walking behind the cart. We got out, too, during some of the descents. The weight of the cart would suddenly thrust against the harness on the old mare's hindquarters – harness called locally 'the breechins' – and it seemed possible that as she held back, slithering and sliding, the cart might overturn. It never did, slightly to my disappointment. Even then I had a nose for the truffles of sensational stories.

The purpose of our expedition was to gather sphagnum moss, which at the time, owing to a shortage of cottonwool, was in demand as a field dressing for wounded soldiers. The most plentiful supply of sphagnum in the parish, according to one knowledgeable kirk elder, was to be found in Barney's Moss. The elder was right. Scraping and pulling for hour after dreary hour, like coolies in a rice field – pictures of whom I had seen in the Church of Scotland magazine, *Life and Work* – we filled four big sacks with the stuff and hoisted them into the cart. The only relief – for me – was a picnic organized by my mother. The ladies drank tea brewed up on a fire of heather twigs augmented by small pieces of dried peat gathered from disused workings nearby. As a special treat I had a bottle of lemonade, a bottle which, to my delight, had a small glass ball for a stopper. (Neil MacLean would have to look out next time we played marbles. I now possessed a glessie.) During the day we saw buzzards flying overhead and another great bird, gliding high above the distant cliffs, which my mother said was a golden eagle.

It was almost dark when we reached home. I was tired and bored with the ladies' chatter. My only consolation was the thought that if my father, fighting in some savage Grecian glade, happened to be wounded, perhaps some of the moss we had gathered that afternoon might save his life. Telling nobody, I began to write a story along such lines. But I soon gave it up. Describing even imaginary wounds on my father's body made me feel sick. And afraid.

The road to the Mull was not contructed until 1830, though the lighthouse itself had been built in 1787–88.

The Mull of Kintyre lighthouse is often referred to in guidebooks – and by authors who should know better – as a 'Stevenson light'. This is not true, though, as they say in the panel games, there is a 'Stevenson connection'.

In 1786 a body of nineteen persons known as the Northern Lighthouse Trustees was set up by an act of parliament. It still exists under the original constitution but is now called the Northern Lighthouse Board (NLB). This body decided that four new lighthouses should be built: at Kinnaird Head near Fraserburgh, at North Ronaldshay in the Orkneys, at Eilean Glas in Scalpay, Harris, and at the Mull of Kintyre. Casting about for a good lighting engineer to do the work, they found Thomas Smith, originally a lampmaker in Edinburgh, who accepted the contract with enthusiasm, even though his promised remuneration was scant and sometimes slow in coming.

Soon he encountered daunting problems. He employed as an assistant George Sheills, 'a mason well recommended', along with two other Edinburgh tradesmen, John and William Purdie. They tackled the Mull lighthouse first, in July 1787, because bad weather was making journeys to the islands difficult and 'at least the Mull was on the mainland'.

Smith had already been warned by the Provost of Campbeltown, himself a Lighthouse Trustee, that much money and time would be required 'to contract for a building in a place so difficult of access and so remote'. He found the warning to be true. Building materials could not be landed at the Mull itself because of the violent tides and 'the steep, 250-foot cliff' on which the lighthouse was to be erected. Everything, therefore, had to be made up into 'tiny parcels' and conveyed by packhorses from Campbeltown seventeen miles away. In his reports, Smith refers to 'rough, trackless moorland and mountainous paths' so dangerous that a horse could make only one journey in a day and that with a load of less than a hundredweight.

Nevertheless, by the end of November George Sheills and the Purdies had built the keeper's house and most of the tower. (Sheills earned 4s. 2d. for 'each lawful day's work', the Purdies 3s.) Meanwhile, Smith had got the lamp and reflectors ready in Edinburgh, but 'with wintry storms now buffeting Kintyre, it was decided to defer shipping the precious light until the spring, and Sheills and the Purdies were recalled home.'

In April of the following year Thomas Smith and his masons returned to the Mull and by June, with the help of some local workers, had completed the tower and installed the light. Each of the reflectors, designed by Smith, was formed of 350 facets of mirror glass one-sixteenth of an inch thick, set in plaster on brass plates. Smith also made sure that a high wall was built between the lighthouse and the cliff edge, 'to prevent the keeper or any of his family from being blown over by the strong winds'.

It was some time, however, before a keeper could be appointed and settled in with plenty of provisions for the winter months, during which, in Smith's words, he would be 'totally removed from society and frequently employed in winning peats for fuel'. But at last, in October, the lantern was officially lit. Since then, undergoing modifications and reconstruction along the years, it has never ceased flashing a warning to ships heading into or out of the North Channel.

Soon after the building of the Mull lighthouse Thomas Smith took as an assistant Robert Stevenson, the nineteen-year-old son of a widow whose maiden name had been Jean Lillie.

Jean Lillie's first husband was a dashing young Glasgow merchant called Alan Stevenson, who, during a business expedition to the West Indies in 1774, died of a fever in St Christopher (now St Kitts), leaving her alone and almost penniless with a two-year-old son. Soon afterwards she married a certain James Hogg, a Glasgow manufacturer about whom almost nothing is known, except that in 1778, whether on account of death or divorce, Jean was no longer married to him. Jean and her son then moved to Edinburgh, where, through meetings at church, they became friends with Thomas Smith and his first wife, Elizabeth, and their two children, Jane and James. They remained friends with the Smith family during the years when Thomas's first wife died of whooping cough and his second, Mary Jack, died of tuberculosis after having given birth to a daughter, Mary Ann.

During Thomas's long absences from home, on lighthouse business, Jean Stevenson (who never referred to herself as Jean Hogg) looked after his fatherless children; and when her own son Robert began looking for employment, declining interest in Latin and Greek having caused him to give up the idea of becoming a minister of the Kirk, it was natural that he should be invited by Thomas Smith to enter his workshop as an apprentice. He became so apt and enthusiastic a pupil that in 1791 he was appointed chief assistant and partner in the business.

In the summer of 1792 he was sent to instal a reflector light at the dangerous entrance to Portpatrick harbour, the Scottish end of the postal service in Ireland. This was his first independent job and marked the beginning of the Stevenson family's long, devoted and widely known involvement with the building of lighthouses. The fact that Robert's first instinct was to be a clergyman, with a care for souls, may indicate the origin of his and his successors' deep concern for the safety of seamen.

That same year Thomas Smith and Jean Stevenson were married. At forty-one she was an ideal partner. She knew his children as well and loved them almost as much as her own son; she shared his religious beliefs and could be depended upon to care for the young folk while he travelled about the country on lighthouse business.

In 1799 a final link was forged in the close family alliance. Robert Stevenson married Jane Smith, the girl who for so many years had been his playmate. It was a happy marriage which produced a daughter, Jane, and four sons, Alan, Bob, David and Thomas. Thomas, the youngest, was the father of Robert Louis Stevenson (whose middle name, incidentally, was always pronounced 'Lewis' by the family, because in fact, long before a kind of literary snowblindness crept in, he was christened 'Lewis'.) From David are descended the contemporary generations, including the novelist, D. E. Stevenson.

Lighthouses and books. Signals flashing in the dark from a family whose loving care for others has always been well matched by their energy and skill in their chosen professions.

It all began with Thomas Smith, the pioneer of modern lighthouse building in Scotland. But in spite of the fact that he was well known to the public in his time, nobody seems to be sure what he looked like. All that R.L.S. could discover about his great-grandfather's personal appearance was contained in the words of an old lighthouse-keeper: 'A tall, stout man coming ashore with a gun over his arm.'

In 1830, when a decision was made to build a road to the Mull of Kintyre, Robert Stevenson's son, David, was put in charge of the work. He brought men and horses from Edinburgh (but also engaged some local labour), and while the road gradually took shape, in general following the direction of the old bridle paths, he lived for six weeks in one of the crofthouses which at the time lay scattered along the wild coastline. But even then the Duke of Argyll was relentlessly depopulating the crofts in order to make way for sheep. For the past hundred years the Mull has been a wilderness almost entirely empty of people: and today archaeologists study the mouldering ruins of the little crofting townships with the same passionless regard as they do the Iron Age duns and Neolithic chambered cairns which are also to be found near the lighthouse.

Before the road was finished David Stevenson had to face at least one unexpected crisis. One of his workmen died of cholera. This caused the entire labour force to down tools and flee to Campbeltown, putting the local population into a considerable state of panic. Helped by his assistant from Edinburgh, a young man called David Rome, David buried the unfortunate victim in a lonely spot at the Mull, far from human habitation. Then, showing an example by himself staying on at the work site, he spent many hours trying to persuade his men and the people of Campbeltown that no danger of infection existed. In the end he succeeded. The road building went on.

When, in 1917, I accompanied my mother and her Guild ladies to the Mull the road was in much the same rough condition as it had been when David Stevenson completed his task. For over a hundred years it had remained a private road, owned and serviced by the Northern Lighthouse Board. After the Second World War, however, all of it except the last swooping, corkscrew mile down to the station was taken over by Argyll County Council, which gave it a coat of tarmac to tempt adventurous tourists. And tempting it has proved. In the first year after the record of 'Mull of Kintyre' was released 3500 people – including Europeans, Americans, Asians and Africans – signed the visitors' book at the lighthouse.

Thomas Smith and David Stevenson would have rejoiced in the interest aroused by the lighthouse and the road. Possibly, however, it remains a matter of indifference to the cholera man who occupies a lonely grave, far from the road and difficult to find. About the place there is a kind of cosmic loneliness: a trough in a tumbling sea of heather, smooth and green like the lee side of a wave. The wind whines over it; and the peewits and the whaups (curlews) fly with the wind, calling to unseen companions. The grave is marked by a single bare stone. It is seldom visited by strangers.

But somebody cares, and the loneliness is not absolute. The last time I made a pilgrimage to this secret sepulchre a bunch of wild flowers lay fading on the stone.

*

The high aseptic savagery of the Mull gives way suddenly to low green hills and fields in the hinterland of Southend.

Today parts of the Mull and some of the uncultivated glens are covered with spruce and fir, planted there by private owners and by the Forestry Commission; but sixty years ago few trees existed in the parish. West wind constantly blustering in from the Atlantic makes it difficult to grow them and, in any case, farmers and shepherds have always regarded trees as useless encumbrances. In their opinion dry stane dykes – as mortarless stone walls are called in Scotland – provide adequate shelter for flocks and herds.

One or two clumps of ash and sycamore were – and still are – to be seen in odd corners on the arable farms; but almost all of these were planted to cover the deep graves of cattle slaughtered during outbreaks of anthrax. (Thanks to stringent regulations and inspections, anthrax is now practically unknown in Scotland, as is bovine tuberculosis.)

When Neil MacLean and I were young only two sizable plantations existed for our pleasure. They were situated on either side of the Con water near the Manse; and from Neil I learned they had been planted by the Duke of Argyll, his father's employer, as cover for the game birds – grouse pheasant, woodcock – hunted by the ducal shooting tenants.

These plantations still exist. But now they are untended, unkempt, like old rubbish dumps. The duke no longer owns the ground on which they stand. In 1955 his predecessor sold off almost all his farms and houses in Kintyre to the sitting tenants, in order to meet an accumulation of debts. The shooting and fishing rights came into the hands of farmers more concerned with the rearing of profitable cattle than with the sheltering and preserving of sometimes highly expensive game. So the plantations decay, the game birds decrease in numbers (mainly owing to disease) and rich business men, carrying double-barrelled shot-guns and wearing knickerbocker suits in startling checks, have ceased to make their autumnal visits to Southend. Were Neil's gamekeeper father alive today he would long ago have added his name to the list of the sad unemployed. (In any case, even though our plantations and moors were kept in good condition, would many business men from the south – of native British origin that is – be able to afford a shooting at £5000 a day, which is the rental for some moors for which figures are available, or handmade guns selling in London at £20,000 a pair?)

But for Neil and me – and our brothers, as they grew older – the larger of these plantations, which lay across the river, was a playground of delight, even though, strictly speaking, we committed trespass every time we entered it.

In winter and early spring the ground beneath the trees was soggy and wet, and we sank in it up to our ankles. At such times our visits were infrequent, though occasionally we found an eerie pleasure in standing silent in a woodland aisle, aware of the dank, earthy smell of winter and surrounded by tall, gaunt trees like cathedral pillars which sheltered us from the wind moaning among their tops. The experience resembled our life in the Mull of Kintyre, I think: a little frightening in its stark remoteness but not so frightening as the chill intimations of a different kind of life outside and beyond, of which we had only a vague comprehension.

In late spring and summer, however, when the ground was dry and fallen twigs cracked sharply beneath our feet, when leaves were bursting out in hanging bundles of green, this was the time for our happiest 'plantin' ploys'. There were birds' nests to find and brightly coloured eggs to blow, with pin holes pierced at either end by trembling, nervous fingers. There were rabbits and grouse and woodcock to spring unexpectedly from under our feet and cause us momentary alarm and abiding pleasure. There were swathes of primroses and wild blue hyacinths (which we called bluebells) and a certain small clearing where wild raspberries grew. The raspberries tasted dry and sour, but we ate them with relish because, on two counts, they were forbidden fruit. First, they belonged to the Duke of Argyll. Secondly, our parents had issued orders that no wild berries of any sort should pass our lips.

We regarded the clearing as our secret headquarters; and as each of our brothers joined us in the plantation he was taken to it, blindfold, and then made to promise, on pain of

terrible physical punishment – even of hanging from a rafter
in one of the Manse outhouses – never to betray its existence
to anyone, not even to the Duke of Argyll, should he
suddenly appear to accuse us of trespass and make us his
prisoners.

The clearing with the wild raspberries is still there; but
today the boys of Southend know nothing about it. The
plantation is not approachable by car. Even for me the
glamour of the place has diminished. Fallen trees, rotten
with acrid-smelling fungus, lie on the turf and block the way
through; and I am sad that its fresh innocence has vanished.
But the sadness does not last long. Memories remain, and
they are real, like small intimations of man's immortality.

If I had the courage I would collect a few of my OAP
contemporaries – sadly not including Neil, who died many
years ago – and spend afternoons in the plantation, crawling
among the undergrowth, plaiting twigs together to make
snares and manufacturing bows and arrows out of hazel
branches and string, in a satisfying game of Cowboys and
Red Indians.

Instead, I sometimes go alone to collect wood for our
living-room fire. We have night storage heaters, that expensive brood sired by a con trick out of government ineptitude;
but Jean insists she would be unhappy without a coal and log
fire to sit at on winter evenings. My daily exercise, therefore,
includes chopping or sawing wood found in the plantation or
washed up on the seashore. I have learned to pick and hoard
the right kinds of wood for a glowing fire and can vouch for
the truth of the old rhyme:

> Beechwood fires are bright and clear
> If the logs are kept a year.
> Chestnut's only good, they say,
> If for long 'tis stored away.
> Birch and fir logs burn too fast
> Blaze up bright and do not last.
> It is by the Irish said
> Hawthorn makes the sweetest bread.
> Elmwood burns like churchyard mould,

E'en the very flames are cold.
Poplar gives a bitter smoke,
Fills your eyes and makes you choke.
Apple wood will scent your room
With an incense like perfume.
Oak and maple, if dry and old,
Keep away the winter cold.
But ash wood wet or ash wood dry
A king shall warm his slippers by.

So does Jean. And so do I.

Florrie Nail lived alone in a wooden hut by the riverside, a few hundred yards downstream from the plantation.

Her real name was Florence MacNeil; but in Southend, as in many another west-coast parish of mixed Highland, Lowland and Irish population, we are inclined to be lazy and drop the 'Mac'. As further examples, Archie MacInnes becomes Erchie Eenis; John MacShannon becomes Joannie Shenak; Margaret MacEachran becomes Peggy Kechran. I suppose that one reason for this habit is that the local versions glide more easily across the tongue. But, of course, 'Nail', 'Eenis', 'Shenak' and 'Kechran' are all approximate reversions, in pronunciation, to the old original Gaelic names. With a 'Mac' before each they mean respectively 'child of Neil,' 'child of Angus', 'child of the storyteller' and 'child of the horseman'. It is interesting to observe that the MacShannons, plentiful in Kintyre, are still, as a family, superb singers and storytellers and that the MacEachrans, inhabitants of the peninsula for two thousand years, are still experts in the handling of farm animals.

Florrie Nail was a good friend of us boys. She was between sixty and seventy years of age when we knew her: ancient in our eyes and indeed much older looking, on account of her dress and a stooping posture caused by hard physical labour and the onset of rheumatism, than sixty-year-old ladies are today. In Florrie's time youthful fashions for grand-mothers were frowned upon as vanities of vanities, bad for the soul, and the national health service was but a gleam in Lloyd George's caring eye.

Florrie's clothes were bundled about her from chin to heavily booted feet, revealing nothing of the body beneath, unlike my mother's smart blouses and hobble skirts. They were of thick black material, so rumpled that it often occurred to Neil and me to wonder if she ever took them off. Her dark-skinned face, framed in long wisps of iron-grey hair, was broad and gaunt. Most of her teeth were missing, and she spoke in a husky voice which often became submerged in bouts of bronchial coughing. Sometimes she smoked tobacco in a broken-stemmed clay pipe, but this was only when some neighbour (like my father) presented her with an ounce of 'thick black'.

Her wooden hut, painted light grey and consisting of a single room, was raised a foot above the turf on four corner posts. Her heating came from an iron stove, its rickety tin chimney emerging from the corrugated iron roof like a drunken question mark. It burned wood and peats and sometimes coal, and on it she cooked porridge and broth and boiled water in a skillet (or shallow pan) for countless cups of strong tea. Her light was furnished during the day by two small windows (placed oddly high up under the eaves so that she couldn't see out of them) and at night time by a cruisie (a small dish of oil with a wick in it). She had two wooden chairs, one for herself and one for visitors whom she considered important. Her bed was a low bunk attached to the wall.

Neil and I usually sat on the wooden floor while she talked to us in a high-pitched voice, which often broke when she had to cough, about people and events in the parish. Sometimes she would spread butter, with a thumb, on high-edged 'dollar' biscuits and present us with one each. We enjoyed her talk and the dollar biscuits and were unaffected by the heavy smell of wood smoke and tobacco and homespun garments and bedclothes which always filled the hut. I believe now that in her turn she enjoyed our company.

She had a small garden in which she grew kale and parsley. Neighbouring farmers allowed her to collect occasional turnips and cabbages from their fields in addition to making sure that she had adequate supplies of butter and cheese. Unknown to the shooters, Neil's father left rabbits and hares on her doorstep. Her monetary income was half a crown a week, poor relief from the parish council.

In Southend today an old lady in a similar situation has a comfortable council house, an old age pension, a supplementary pension, a television set, regular visits from a doctor or a nurse and an ambulance service to convey her to a hospital in Campbeltown should she require specialized medical treatment. If she takes flu, in spite of an annual 'flu jag', or contracts any other temporary illness, a home help attends her domestic needs. Assistance in the administration of her social needs is provided by the church (often through the Woman's Guild), the Women's Rural Institute and the community council.

The minister of the parish was Florrie Nail's only regular visitor. The minister today visits her modern counterpart and is grateful that the Christian ideals of love and care have flowered to such an extent that his burden and concern is shared by many others, making it so much lighter than that of his predecessor.

In my childhood the old folk in Southend, like Florrie, inhabited huts and noisome village hovels, cast up like flotsam on the beaches of old age. But they all possessed one characteristic which continually aroused my boyish admiration. This was a tough independence of spirit, a courage in the face of want and deprivation which seemed incredible to Neil and me, happed around as we were – according to the standards of the time at any rate – with every physical and moral support. And Florrie Nail possessed another characteristic which caused us to shiver in our sandshoes.

We were prowling in the plantation one summer afternoon, pioneering a new route through heavy undergrowth to the clearing. We kept a sharp lookout for Indians, snakes and tigers and froze into immobility when any recognizable sound occurred which could be construed in imagination as threatening danger. We were confident there was no danger among the tall trees; but we could achieve full enjoyment only by creating the idea of it in our minds. Green twigs brushed our faces. Our knees were scratched by bramble thorns and smeared with damp, acrid-smelling leaf mould. Sunshine glinted through the treetops and shadows flickered with thrilling menace when the treetops moved in the wind.

Suddenly we heard a heavy sound – a sound we were unable immediately and instinctively to identify and which caused us spasms of real terror. Neil flattened himself so close to the ground that when after a moment he raised his head one cheek was covered with leaf mould, like a Hallowe'en mask.

We waited. The leaves of a rhododendron bush in front of us were trembling. What terrible creature crouched behind them, ready to spring at our throats?

Without warning a face appeared in the midst of the bush. A hawklike female face with a wide mouth – a mouth which suddenly uttered a heart-stopping screech. I had heard my father preach about the witch of Endor. Was this a witch of Southend, intent upon casting a spell on Neil and me, turning us perhaps into toadstools or even pillars of salt?

We lay there, desperately afraid but incapable of any physical action. And then the rhododendron branches parted and through them stepped Florrie Nail, cackling with laughter.

'I gi'ed ye a fricht, boys! I gi'ed ye a fricht!'

Our relief was so great that I, for one, was ready to howl and shed tears. But Neil was made of harder stuff. He scrambled to his feet.

'Ye bloody auld bitch!' he shouted at her. 'Whit are ye daein' in the plantin'?'

By the age of ten all Southend schoolboys (including the minister's sons) had acquired a substantial repertoire of swearwords. Florrie, therefore was unsurprised by Neil's outburst.

'Trackin' ye doon. Fur a tare!' she screeched, bursting again into banshee laughter. 'I used tae play here in the plantin' masel' when I was a lassie. I was gey guid at the trackin', and I jeest wunnert if I could still dae it. Ye never heard me, did ye?'

'Fur a tare', in our local dialect, means 'for a joke'. For

Neil and me, however, it was no joke. Pride in our courage and manly skills as hunters had been gravely undermined; and the knowledge that an old woman like Florrie had outmanoeuvred us and scared us almost out of our wits was hard to stomach. But Neil, as usual, was able quickly to adjust to the situation and make the best of it.

He laughed. 'Ach, we heard ye a' richt. We were jeest playin' alang wi' ye.'

I have always been able to accept with alacrity any excuses offered by friends for my mistakes and errors of judgement. Neil's brave words made me feel happier at once.

'What about another game, Florrie?' I said. 'You hide and we'll try to track *you* down.'

'Richt ye are,' she said with delight. 'Jeest gi'e me five meenits. Then ye can come efter me.'

At the end of the afternoon she took us back to the hut, where she gave us tea and dollar biscuits.

As a boy I lacked the wit to identify Florrie's reasons for coming to play with us in the plantation; but now, being even older than she was at the time, I can understand them very well.

About a year later, Florrie died of influenza. Her hut remained empty for a time, rotting and crumbling in the wind and rain. In November 1918, soon after the signing of the Armistice, there occurred a day and night of heavy rain when the river Con roared down from the hills in a brown flood. Some of the trees in the plantation were broken and swept away. Florrie's hut was lifted from its supports. At high speed it leaped and rolled downstream, eventually crashing against a stone bridge and splintering into a hundred pieces. Part of the bridge collapsed and a ten-foot gap yawned in the road.

I was seedy and swollen with mumps at the time. When Neil and I went to inspect the damage I had on a balaclava helmet which my father had worn in Salonika. Perhaps it was my debilitated condition which made me feel like crying when I thought of Florrie and her hut, both gone for ever.

Was she a spinster or a widow? Was she a native of

Southend, or a traveller who had come to visit and decided to stay? Had she relatives in Kintyre?

I knew none of the answers then. I still don't know. Nobody is old enough to remember and tell me.

3. Downstairs, Upstairs

Florrie Nail was only one of the many characters who, sixty years ago, shared in the life of Southend.

My aged contemporaries are inclined to complain that no such characters exist today. This is partly true in the sense that the welfare state has helped to do away with real poverty and also to alleviate many of the diseases, both mental and physical, which handicapped old age in the early part of the century. Better education has tended to smooth out the oddities which attracted us to people older than ourselves, and television has made less urgent the search by youth for enlightenment and amusement from their older neighbours.

But I keep reminding my friends among the OAPs that their complaints may not be entirely valid. Young people today live in a different world: a world of technological wonder gradually merging into another of the microchip. They may look upon us old squares, digging in our heels against the pull of the twenty-first century, in much the same was as Neil and I looked upon the Florrie Nails of our time. Some of *us* may be the characters about whom a budding author, now concealed in our midst, will write books in the years to come.

Not long ago this idea was strengthened in my mind when from my favourite armchair in the clubhouse I saw my son Jock and a friend of his – unaware that I was watching – doubled up with laughter on the eighteenth green while another young man, shaping up to a three-foot putt, suddenly leaped inches into the air and hysterically prodded the ball past the hole by several yards. It dawned on me that this was an exact demonstration of my method of putting (since the 'over-sixty yipps' afflicted me) and that it was being done with deliberate intent to amuse. Afterwards I said nothing to anybody, not even to Jock. But I remembered how Neil and I and the other boys had often put into mocking action the foibles of *our* characters.

The children of a Scottish manse are privileged. They are brought up in the knowledge not only of the love of God but also of the fear of God which engenders self-discipline. They learn, too, by reason of contact with visitors to the manse of every sort and condition, not to be snobs or, which is as bad, anti-snobs.

As a small boy I knew and was able to communicate with, for example, Geordie the odd-job man, Danny the Tink, and Ina, Dowager Duchess of Argyll; Hughie MacKay the drainer, and Mrs Boyd of Carskiey, who was a millionairess; Big Doser and Kleek, Mrs Galbraith in the wee shop, and Robert Ralston, the prosperous farmer who was also a ruling elder. I knew and sometimes visited Jamie Doyle who lived rough with a woman companion in a cave above Kilmashenachan shore.

My parents treated them all as equal in the sight of God and made no difference in the quality of their hospitality. When the occasion arose they all got tea from my mother and some of her own locally renowned home-baked scones. Then, again if appropriate, my father would take them into his study to discuss their business and dispense benign encouragement or forthright criticism as he saw fit. He had words as readily with the Dowager Duchess as with Danny the Tink and commanded the respect of both.

There were some who refused to enter the drawing-room and, indeed, would only come inside as far as the kitchen on a cold day. Those were the tinkers, or 'travelling people' as they are now called by sensitive social workers: the Townsleys and the Williamsons who for generations made Kintyre their happy hunting ground. (They still do, though today many of them live in council houses.) But it was the tinkers who laid down the rules, not the minister or his wife.

As a result of all this I grew up almost unaware of the class distinction which I now realize was widespread, even in the remoteness of Kintyre, before the levelling influence of the two world wars and of preaching politicians like Keir Hardie. I am thankful for it. Having to calculate the warmth – or coolness – of your approach to another human being must cause difficult mental and moral problems, and I am an advocate of the simple and uncomplicated life in which you can always be yourself and never need to act a part.

Though learning to respect him as an individual, I disliked and was scared of Geordie, our occasional gardener. I was also, in a way, scared of Danny the Tink, an old man with brown, weathered features so aquiline that his nose and chin seemed ready to touch every time he champed his toothless jaws. He looked like a cunning wizard in one of my picture books.

When I knew him, he lived alone in a two-roomed cottage in the village, though in the mirky past, on the road as a tinker, he had fathered a family. A married daughter sometimes came to do washing for him and to tidy up, as best she could, the dull, dank rooms, which, even on a summer's day, required the light of a candle or paraffin lamp.

The cottage was one of a row of broken-down buildings, like decaying teeth, which had once been thatched but were now roofed with rusty corrugated iron. The place had no official designation but was nicknamed locally Teapot Lane. This may have been because the cobbled pavement outside the front doors sloped down to an open drain into which tealeaves, fish heads and even human excreta were often thrown. The furnishings of each cottage were incomplete without a heavily sprung rat trap.

In his younger days, as well as being a tinker selling and repairing pots and pans, Danny had done a great deal of casual labour on the farms, especially during the sowing season and at harvest time. But he disliked the idea of permanent work. He was tall and strong and, with the best of them, could dig hill drains, plough straight with a 'high-cutter' and toss cornsheaves powerfully on to ladder-sided carts. While it lasted his work was regular and faithful. He had no taste for drink and never went on the spree like so many of the farm workers of his day, desperate to forget,

even for an hour or two, the unrelenting dawn-to-dusk
labour to which they were condemned. But Danny had his
own peculiar weakness. Suddenly he would tire of effort and
tell the farmer he had to go. Confiding in nobody, he would
disappear for many weeks, though rumours might circulate
that he'd been seen in faraway and, to us, outlandish places –
such as Arrochar and Inveraray – in the company of tinkers.

Danny, however, always returned to Southend and,
because he was a good worker, usually found employment on
some farm and a place to sleep in an attic or an outhouse.

When he became old and the fires of travel lust began to
cool, he was given the house in Teapot Lane by the parish
council. Instead of labouring on the farms, he augmented his
weekly half a crown poor relief as a repairer of clocks and
watches.

His reputation was made by work he did on a famous old
grandfather clock in Brunerican, Jean's family home. Years
before it had been brought there from another farm in the
parish, in an iron-shod cart drawn by a Clydesdale mare. The
cabinet containing the main works and the round white face
(hand-painted with scenes depicting the four seasons) had
been laid carefully on a pile of straw; but the pendulum had
been removed so that it could be held aloft throughout the
journey by a devoted old woman sitting in the cart to ensure
that at no time did it 'go off the plumb'. Despite all
precautions, however, something had gone wrong, and for
many years in Brunerican the clock refused to go. Then
Danny came along, searched its entrails with a candle and set
to work. Within a few hours, to general amazement, the
clock was ticking and striking the hours with healthy emphasis. Seventy years later it is still going, worth a great deal of
money, I believe, and a memorial to Danny's skill.

Small clocks and watches were taken away by Danny to
work upon in his home. How his ancient eyes coped with
their intricate interiors was a puzzle to Neil and me. Sometimes we sat on the wooden floor, watching. A dumpy,
one-wick paraffin lamp burned by his elbow, on a table
littered with tiny wheels and springs, small screwdrivers and
delicate tweezers. He wore wire-rimmed spectacles and, as

he worked, held the clocks and watches only an inch or two away from them. Every so often the spectacles would begin to slide down the long, pointed nose. Then he would straighten up, adjust them carefully and, with a muttered Gaelic curse, resume the operation. The whole picture comes back to me now, like a study by an old Dutch master.

Danny's last illness struck him down soon after the outbreak of the First World War. The Padre sat at one side of the straw bed, while the daughter, a widow now of almost seventy whose name was Phemie, sat on the other. A candle stood in its wax on a packing case, its flame flickering in the draught from a window stuffed with rags.

The night crept into morning, and my father shivered in his overcoat.

The slow breaths became shallower. 'It's his time,' whispered the daughter.

Danny was moving painfully, trying to speak. The Padre heard the words: 'The earth, Phemie. The earth.'

On the mantelpiece was a saucer containing a white-brown mixture. The daughter looked at the saucer, then at my father. He nodded.

She took it and laid it on her father's breast, carrying out, by means of the earth and the salt, an ancient pagan ritual for death.

And then, as the Padre prayed, the withered flesh ceased to move and the shallow breathing stopped.

The earth and the salt. The bread and the wine. Is there a difference?

Teapot Lane no longer exists. In place of the seven or eight small dark cottages there are three private houses and a modern store. Hygiene is maintained at a high standard.

But there is nobody in Southend today who can repair a watch or a grandfather clock.

With my parents I visited Danny the Tink in his unsavoury 'but and ben'. I also accompanied them when they went for lunch – as happened fairly frequently – to the mansion house of Carskiey. (In the bay below the house, some distance from the shore, there lies a half-submerged rock shaped like a bird's wing. In the Gaelic it is called Carraig Sgeith, the winged rock. Hence Carskiey.)

Mrs Boyd was an elderly widow, small and round and sombrely dressed like Queen Victoria, one of the Coats family whose fortunes derived from the thread mills of Paisley. She was a millionairess, a fact which we bandied about amongst ourselves with quiet awe. According to the stories her father was so rich that when his numerous family was young he and his wife often hired a train for the holidays, in which, with a multitude of servants, they visited not only many parts of Britain but the Continent as well.

Neil and I spent many an interesting hour in the Manse attics speculating on what we should do with a million pounds. Neil's most bizarre idea must have occurred to him soon after the outbreak of the First World War. This was to manufacture a huge gun, to be placed on top of Tapoc, the 700-feet-high volcanic rim which overlooks the village: a gun so powerful that it could hurl a shell all the way to Berlin.

'I'd aim it at the Kaiser's palace,' he said. 'If we kilt *him* the bloody Germans wad soon stop fechtin'!'

My own instant reaction to the acquisition of a million pounds would have been to purchase a brand new bicycle with a three-speed gear. I also considered buying Southend and declaring it a separate kingdom, with the Padre as king, of course, and myself as heir to the throne. And with Neil, as he grew older, as my prime minister. But when my parents once put the question to me, I was cunning enough to strike a note neither worldly nor material.

'I'd give it to the poor,' I told them, unctuously, adding as a small salve to conscience, 'Most of it, anyway.'

'Ay, you have the right way of it,' my father said, obviously gratified that his eldest son should harbour such staunch Christian ideals.

My mother, saying nothing, looked at me with the small sidelong smile which I learned later indicated scepticism. But her silence did not worry me. I knew that no matter what I said or did she would still love me.

A great oblong pile of masonry turreted with scores of chimneys, Carskiey had only recently been built (in 1905) and contained every kind of amenity described as 'modern' at the time. For example, salt water baths then being considered essential to good health, all the bathrooms were piped to receive water pumped up from the sea half a mile away and heated by coal-fired boilers. There was electricity, generated in a small building at the back of the house from which there issued hummings and whinings much to my youthful taste. (It was to be another forty years before the North of Scotland Hydro-Electric Board brought electricity to the general public in Southend.) The tall french windows at the front of the house opened on to a paved patio of enormous extent. Not long ago an architect told me that today the paving alone of such an area would cost approximately £100,000. With trees and garden bushes sheltering it on three sides I have always thought it would make a wonderful stage for an open-air presentation of *A Midsummer Night's Dream*.

My first visit to Carskiey remains clear in my memory.

Mrs Boyd sent a car to collect us: a dignified Daimler with studded tyres. Those tyres caused me some anxiety. I knew they were pneumatic. Was it not possible, therefore, that the studs, if hammered into the rubber in the same way as tackets into boots, would eventually work their way in and burst the inner tubes? Lacking, as people often remind me, a proper scientific education, I am still vague as to how those flat, highly polished metal studs were fixed in the rubber, and, indeed, as to their value in strengthening the tyres.

My father and mother sat in the rear, the Daimler's hood folded back because the day was fine, their knees covered by a tartan rug. I sat beside the chauffeur. Apart from my worry about the tyres, I enjoyed the run from the Manse to Carskiey. Though the distance was only about four miles, it took us at least twenty minutes. (After all, the days were not long past when a motorcar had to be preceded by a person waving a red flag.) We met farm carts on the way. The horse in one of them reared and plunged at the sound of the Daimler's engine and had to be taken off the road and held steady as we passed. But the main reason for my enjoyment was a conversation with the Cockney chauffeur, whose uninhibited language, when my ear became attuned to the accent, was greatly to my liking.

As we passed a cottage in which the occupants, a young man and his wife, were said to have quarrelled bitterly in public over the past few days, I ventured a phrase I had picked up from a book.

'A rift in the lute there,' I said.

He grinned. 'More like a lute in the wrong rift,' he told me in a hoarse whisper, so that my parents could not hear.

Hours later, that night as I lay in bed, the meaning of his diagnosis occurred to me. It was an important addition to my education as a man of the world.

The chauffeur stopped the car at Carskiey's main entrance. He sprang from the driving seat, polished leather leggings twinkling in the sunlight, hurried to the rear, lifted the rug from my parents' knees and handed my mother out. Then, precisely timed, the great oaken doors opened, like curtains on a stage, revealing a tall, handsome butler wearing immaculate tails. Slowly, like an actor, he descended the shallow steps and greeted us with a bow. Finally, dismissing the chauffeur and the car with a gesture, he led us into the house.

Having dealt personally with the Padre's coat and hat and my school cap, while a maid in a black dress and white apron fussed around my mother in a side room, he preceded us along wide, softly carpeted corridors to the drawing-room. Opening the door and using his voice as unctuously as any minister, he announced, 'The Reverend Angus John and Mrs MacVicar. And Master Angus.' (He was a Scot and knew, of course, that to refer to my father as the Reverend MacVicar would be to reveal social ignorance: social ignorance similar to that of the American who, in the distant future, was to address a prime minister as Sir Churchill.) I liked the 'Master Angus' bit. In an age when small boys were encouraged to be neither seen nor heard, it gave me an unusual sense of importance.

Mrs Boyd laid aside an intricate sampler on which she had been working and rose from her rocking chair. My father and mother towered above her, because she wasn't much taller than I was. 'Come, dear people. Please make yourselves comfortable by the fire.'

The fire was huge, containing coals and logs blazing in extravagant profusion. I felt hot even though I sat as far away from it as possible. The room was bright with cascading chintzes and white lace covers. It appeared to me to be chock-full of furniture, flowers and pictures. Scattered about were small tables containing books, papers and magazines. They represented for me, accustomed to comparatively bare rooms in the Manse, highlights of luxury, and I resisted a strong temptation to go and inspect them. The mantelpiece was decorated in white and gilt. Above it hung an oil painting in a gilt frame of an impressive, bearded gentleman who, I suppose, was Mrs Boyd's father.

Chattering with animation about events in the Parish, Mrs Boyd pressed a bell. A footman made an entrance carrying a silver tray of drinks: sherry for my parents, soda water for Mrs Boyd and lemonade, made from fresh lemons and sugar, for me.

For the first time in my life I found ice cubes in my lemonade. It was the most beautiful drink I had ever tasted, and when it was done, in an attempt to prolong the enjoyment, I tried to slide the melting cubes down the side of the glass into my mouth. One of them missed my mouth and, as I spluttered and choked in an effort to retrieve it, fell with a *plop* on the thick carpet.

'Angus!' My mother was mortified.

Mrs Boyd uttered a tinkling little laugh. 'Dear little boy!' she said, while the footman sidled forward with silver tongs to retrieve the ice. He also snatched away my empty glass. The confidence boost of 'Master Angus' was engulfed in a wave of embarrassment.

When the butler announced that luncheon was served, and Mrs Boyd led us into the dining-room, the table at which we sat caused me further embarrassment. It was covered, end to end, with a huge, white tablecloth, a virgin setting for gleaming arrays of cutlery, crystal jugs and glasses, silver condiment dishes and vases of flowers. Arranged before me was an assortment of spoons, knives and forks, the like of which I had never seen before. I decided to play it cool and follow my mother's example in their use, reckoning that my father, never one to show much interest in the fripperies of life, might lead me into a few false moves.

The footman brought plates of soup from the sideboard, where the butler presided over what I know now to have been a kind of electric grill on which there sat various tureens and chafing dishes. I watched my mother. She took the big spoon on her outside-right position. I took the same spoon on mine and essayed a few quiet sips in time with her. Meanwhile, the Padre, having taken a spoon from *above* his plate, was downing his soup with noisy enjoyment, carrying on, at the same time, a discourse directed at his hostess on the subject of bad housing in the village.

Then we were served with something covered in a white parsley sauce which I decided was a kind of fish. Again I watched my mother and found the appropriate knife and fork. I was tempted to use the broad flat of the knife to convey to my mouth the last of the parsley sauce, but a glance from my mother gave me a timely warning. It was a delicious sauce; but it dripped through the prongs of my fork and eventually I had to leave most of it, uneaten. How did this, I wondered, fit in with my mother's frequent injunctions to remember the poor starving boys of Africa and China and eat up every scrap on my plate? Rebellious thoughts stirred in my slightly dazed mind. Had I been eating in the house of Danny the Tink would I have been under such artificial restraint?

Soon my situation appeared to become even more confined and confused. As slices of roast mutton were offered on large warm plates, the butler poured wine into all the glasses except mine.

My father took a swig of it and smacked his lips in appreciation. 'Hock,' he said. 'Nothing like a good hock.'

'I'm so glad, minister,' smiled Mrs Boyd, looking more and more like Queen Victoria. 'I'm not a connoisseur of wine myself.'

'Neither am I, Mrs Boyd. But I like a good hock.'

In passing, I may say that we remembered his taste on

all his birthdays until he was over ninety.

But on that distant day I appeared to have been forgotten and left with nothing to drink. Presently, however, I noticed that on the table in front of me was a white porcelain bowl filled with a clear liquid in which floated small slices of lemon. Was this a new kind of lemonade concocted for my benefit? The receptacle was oddly shaped and perhaps not easy to drink from; but I was thirsty and began stretching out my hand to give it a trial.

I caught my mother's eye. My hand ceased to move. I watched, almost holding my breath, while she dipped her fingers in the bowl which fronted her and then wiped them dry on her napkin.

It was my first introduction to fingerbowls, and I was awestruck. I wondered if even King George and Queen Mary in Buckingham Palace ate their food in such style. But again I took my cue from my mother. Slowly my hand moved forward. I twiddled my fingers in the water and finally wiped them dry on my napkin in what I hoped was a natural, yet sophisticated manner.

Later on I noticed that the Padre completely ignored his fingerbowl except on one occasion when he used it as a repository for some mutton gristle which he had found difficult to chew. I must say I admired his brusque attitude to the prim rules of etiquette and his lack of embarrassment when he broke them. And I was interested to observe that Mrs Boyd appeared not to notice anything wrong and listened closely to his every word as he commented upon various religious and social topics.

In any case, soon after my narrow escape from a humiliating gaffe, the footman was reminded by Mrs Boyd that my glass was empty. He filled it with more lemonade and ice – his nose somewhat in the air, I thought, perhaps due to the memory of the mess I had made on the drawing-room carpet – and I continued to eat my lunch with enjoyment.

Before we went home that afternoon I was left to look at some picture books which Mrs Boyd – as she explained – had purchased specially for the occasion. To my disappointment they were of an improving nature, the text so profuse that it left scarcely any room for the promised pictures. And the pictures themselves, of children dying in the snow, for example, and of drunken fathers driving their offspring into despairing female arms, were so far removed from my own experience of life that, though at first a little upset, I became, after a while, extremely bored.

One particular picture, however, sticks like a burr in my memory. It was of a boy and girl in ragged clothes sprawling in the gutter of a city street. Beside them lay a broken handcart from which a few scrawny herrings had spilled out on to the pavement. Passing by was a smart horse-drawn carriage driven by a gentleman wearing a top hat, whose carelessness had been the obvious cause of the accident. To the sprawling infants and their scattered herrings he paid no attention whatsoever.

Even at the time it occurred to me to compare this cruel indifference to poverty with the concern for the needy shown by Mrs Boyd, whom, as I pretended to read, I could overhear arranging with my parents for various charitable gifts to be made on her behalf. Blankets for old Mrs MacAlpine up the glen, canisters of tea for certain families in Teapot Lane (very appropriate, I thought), parcels of food for the Doyles in Kilmashenachan Cave. But no money for anyone. Mrs Boyd was adamant about that. 'Drink is the curse of the lower classes,' I heard her say. 'We cannot encourage it.'

She used the term 'lower classes' quite naturally, and, I am sure, without derogatory intent. Her concern was always for those less well placed financially than herself, and she voted Liberal all her life. But that evening, in the Manse, before being sent to bed, I heard my father say to my mother, 'I wish Mrs Boyd would go and see those people for herself, instead of leaving everything to us. It would do her and them a lot of good.' He did not refer to 'upper' and 'lower classes' then, nor at any other time.

I suppose it was that day at Carskiey, in spite of the fact that I was less than nine years old, that the divisions in society began to worry me. They still do, sixty-five years later; but answers to the problem remain elusive.

They are elusive, I believe, because people have varying opinions upon what constitutes the good life. It would seem that in the world today, on the evidence of declarations issued by both the so-called Rightists and Leftists – higher profits for the former, higher wages for the latter – the majority of people consider that the good life depends upon the acquisition of more and more money: a situation born of need but nurtured in greed which inevitably leads to inflation and unemployment and thus defeats its own ends. There are others, including the members of various religious and philosophical bodies, who preach the benefits of higher education reinforced by an example of charitable service to others: people who find self-satisfaction not in counting their money but in counting the good deeds they are allowed to perform. But somewhere underneath the pile are those trapped by power politics, those who are both physically and spiritually impoverished, with neither money nor education, and who have no vision whatever of a good life because the clouds of their misery loom so dark.

What *is* the good life? The ancient tale of the search for a happy man, which ended on an island in a peaceful sea inhabited by a greybeard who hadn't even a shirt to put on his back, may have some relevance to the question. So, I think, may a text from the Bible, used first in the Old Testament and repeated in the New: 'Love thy neighbour.' Which does not mean 'Love thy neighbour in theory, at a comfortable distance.'

Sometimes, living in the countryside as I do, working among pleasant people, I try to persuade myself that I have found the good life. But as long as poverty and disease and misery exist in our own and distant lands can *anyone* say he is enjoying a good life?

Every few years I am offered the good life by Socialists, Liberals, Tories and Scottish Nationalists. And now by Social Democrats. I have voted for them all and been disappointed in the results, because their manifestos invariably turn out to have been conceived on a basis of materialism. I cling to an idea given to his students by Professor A. A. Bowman, my old Professor of Moral Philosophy at Glasgow University:

'There is a divinity within every man. Respect and reverence for this divinity is the foundation of civilized behaviour.' May I say that in this idea I also glimpse an answer to the question: 'Who – or what – is God?'

While I was growing up my father was often visited by Robert Ralston, the farmer at Macharioch. When he came, if I was anywhere near the Manse at the time, I made haste to sit in on their conversation. It introduced me to a fascinating subject about which I knew practically nothing.

Robert Ralston was a burly, red-faced man with a high-pitched voice which did not match his size. He liked a dram and looked as if he might be more at home in an agricultural sale ring, with its roaring cattle and dung and dirt and loud badinage between rival bidders, than in the quiet study of a manse. But I soon discovered this was not true. When he called upon the Padre it was to discuss literature: particularly the works of Burns and Shakespeare.

He was the descendant of a long line of Lowland lairds brought to Kintyre in the late seventeenth century by the Duke of Argyll, chief of Clan Campbell. In 1647 the Covenanting Protestant Campbells had seized possession of Kintyre from the Roman Catholic MacDonalds. Many of the Highlanders in the peninsula, followers of the Clan Donald, had been killed or had died of plague or had fled to Ireland, and the duke, killing two birds with one stone, decided to bring to his deserted lands good farmers who would also support his Covenanting activities. The result was that from that time the population of Kintyre became one third Highland, one third Lowland and, on account of age-long comings and goings across the narrow sea, one third Irish.

The first Ralston in Southend was also named Robert. In the graveyard at Kiel the headstones face the east and the rising sun, a custom derived from our sun-worshipping ancestors. But, alone among hundreds, old Robert Ralston's stone faces dourly north, because, according to legend, his last command was that he should be buried with his back to Rome.

His descendant, my father's friend, was more tolerant. His

interests, too, were wider. He studied English literature and
discussed it regularly with my father. This often happened on
a Monday morning while other farmers were attending
markets in Campbeltown but when Robert Ralston knew
that the minister had a day off. I made little sense of what
they talked about; but something in the sound of the poetry
they quoted gave me strange stirrings of excitement.

> Then gently scan your brother man,
>   Still gentler sister woman;
> Tho' they may gang a kennin wrang,
>   To step aside is human.

And again:

> What is love? 'tis not hereafter;
> Present mirth hath present laughter;
>   What's to come is still unsure:
> In delay there lies no plenty;
> Then come kiss me, sweet and twenty,
>   Youth's a stuff will not endure.

These verses, only two among the many tossed about
between the minister and the farmer, have remained in my
memory because of their lilting sound. Years later I came to
understand what they meant, and it is possible their influence
has caused me in the end to write this book. 'Youth's a stuff
will not endure.' But may I not try to prove that youthful
recollection does? With its influence on people for good or
ill.

Recollection has nagging qualities. Robert Ralston's own
education was important to him; but as a member of the
Southend School Board had he as wide a concern for the
education of others? The policy of the board, composed
almost entirely of farmers, never changed. It was that
children should be encouraged to leave school as early as
possible so that the supply of cheap farm labour might be
ensured. Top wages in those days amounted to about £10 in
the half-year. And yet I still possess, in my library, a
well-used copy of *Cassell's Book of Quotations* by W.
Gurney Benham, which Robert Ralston presented to my

father nearly seventy years ago, knowing that a minister's stipend did not make easy the purchase of expensive reference books.

In my privileged position as a minister's son I was able to study society from many angles. It wasn't – and still is not – a comfortable position.

4. Fata Morgana

As boys coming on for eleven years old, Neil and I called him
Old Charlie, though at the time he must only have been in
his middle forties. A casual farm worker, employed mainly
as a drainer and fencer, he had just been demobbed from
army service in the First World War, and his language was
salty. He and his wife had a large family. One day the eldest
boy was overheard by the schoolmaster uttering loud swearwords in the playground. The strap was used, and Charlie
was informed officially of his son's misdemeanour. He was
shocked. He told the schoolmaster, 'I'm bloody sure he never
heard language like that in oor hoose!'

Charlie was rough and ready. He was related distantly to
Big Doser, our enemy, but showed no favouritism on that
account. One evening he stood leaning against the wall of the
hotel coach house – a favourite stance of his – holding court
with Neil and me, a fascinated audience. The subject of his
discourse was sex.

Sixty years ago Clydesdale stallions from 'outside' travelled the district, serving local mares. Whenever we could, Neil
and I were present to witness the coverings, dramatic events
accompanied by much neighing and rearing and clattering of
passion-powered hooves. They caused in us feelings of
excitement which we made no effort to analyse. And they
taught us all we needed to know about the practical side of
sex.

Charlie chuckled as he told us about a stallion which that
day had visited the farm he was working on – the stallion's
name was Dunure Footprint – and described to us how the
Footprint had refused to have anything to do with a
young virgin mare but how happy he had been and how well

he had performed when an old mare whom he'd often covered before had been brought out to him. 'Ay,' Charlie said, shifting the wad of tobacco in his jaw, 'stallions is like men. They ken that the aulder the fiddle the sweeter the tune!'

Neil and I were admiring this pearl of wisdom when suddenly we saw Big Doser and Kleek approaching from the direction of the village. We stopped talking and began to move away.

'Back here!' snarled Charlie.

We stopped.

'Ye've nae spunk!' he said. 'Ye're bloody feart!'

I was only too ready to agree; but Neil said, 'We're no' feart!'

'Ye're runnin' awa',' Charlie told him. 'Turnin' yer back tae the enemy.'

The big farm lads came nearer. Neil didn't move. I stayed beside him, queasy in my stomach.

Big Doser saw us. 'Ye wee cunts!' he roared; and Kleek, wiping 'snotters' from his nose, shrieked, 'Tak the balls aff them!'

They stopped, obviously surprised that we didn't turn tail, as we usually did when they appeared. I wanted to escape, while yet there was time, but Charlie said, 'Stan' yer grun'!' Something in his sergeant-major voice made me obey.

Big Doser glowered at us. He reminded me of a bad-tempered Ayrshire bull, pawing the ground while he made up his mind to charge. Kleek, sniffing and sniffling, looked vicious.

Kleek bent and picked up a stone. Big Doser charged.

We backed away. Charlie put his foot out. In full flight Big Doser tripped over it. Arms spread wide, he sprawled on the cobbles, winded. Kleek, exposed, dropped the stone.

Charlie pulled Big Doser to his feet. 'Lea' the weans alane! If ye want a fight try somebody yer ain bloody size!'

But Neil and I had taken enough. Pride was jettisoned in the interests of safety. We ran off, up the road, as fast as our legs could move.

It had been a rough evening, what with the talk of sex and

the onset of violence. For once we appreciated the peace of our respective homes.

Not long ago, over a sociable dram, I was telling this story to a retired farmer in Southend: a tall spare old man, straight-backed still as when he had served with the Argylls in the First World War, and incredibly, about twenty years older than I was.

'Dunure Footprint,' he mused. 'I remember him well. A son of the famous Baron of Buchlyvie.'

I nearly said, 'So what?' Instead I stayed silent as the warmth of reminiscence glowed in his eyes.

'The Baron travelled in Southend when I was a boy: the best breeding Clydesdale stallion that ever lived, and the most famous. Did you know that a case about him went to the House of Lords?'

'Have another dram,' I said, and soon the memories came to life.

The Baron, I learned, was bought as a two-year-old colt at the Aberdeen Highland Show in 1902. The purchaser was a hard-headed Ayrshire farmer, James Kilpatrick of Craigie Mains. The price he paid was £700, plus a gelding as a kind of 'luckspenny'.

A few months earlier Kilpatrick had sold a prize-winning stallion to his neighbour at Dunure Mains, another dour character called William Dunlop. This stallion had died of an unexpected ailment before being put to work, and to recompense Dunlop for the bad bargain Kilpatrick gave him a half share in the Baron. The deal was made with a hand slap, a custom that still lingers. Nothing was put in writing.

Soon the Baron was fertilizing mares so infallibly and so handsomely that Dunlop made up his mind to become the sole owner. At a Kilmarnock Show, again without putting pen to paper, he persuaded Kilpatrick to part with his share in the stallion for £2000. The Baron was taken at once to Dunlop's farm, Dunure Mains, and a few days later the pair foregathered in the Tam o'Shanter Inn at Ayr to conclude the financial side of the transaction.

It was then that the trouble started. Over their drams

Kilpatrick and Dunlop quarrelled furiously, and intrigued witnesses understood that in the end the deal was called off and an agreement made that the two men should continue to divide the stud fees, with the stallion remaining at Dunure Mains.

In 1904, however, Dunlop stopped paying over Kilpatrick's share and, oddly enough, nothing was said about this by his partner until 1908, when the pair met at a sheep sale. Keenly interested onlookers heard the two men arguing loudly, with Kilpatrick demanding his share of the stud fees which had accumulated over the past·four years. Dunlop shouted back at him that he had no right to any share: he had sold his interest long ago.

While the Baron's production line of foals continued to increase in numbers and profitability Kilpatrick took his case to the Court of Session, where Lord Skerrington, a judge with knowledge not only of the law· but also of Ayrshire farmers and Clydesdale horses, found for Kilpatrick as half-owner.

Grimly Dunlop appealed to the Inner House, where, to everybody's surprise, he won.

But Kilpatrick, determined Ayrshire man that he was, could not stomach defeat. He took the case to the House of Lords; and there, amid a conflagration of publicity which, in Scotland at any rate, equalled that which later accompanied the outbreak of the First World War, he achieved final victory.

Afterwards the fame and fruitfulness of the Baron showed no sign of decreasing. Unfortunately, the arguing and back-biting between the two farmers showed no sign of decreasing either. Bitterness became so acute that eventually some neighbouring farmers, in a bid to salve it, persuaded them to put the Baron up for sale.

But Kilpatrick still did not trust Dunlop, and Dunlop still did not trust Kilpatrick. Each reserved the right to bid; and it was a condition of the sale that the full price had to be paid over before the delivery of the purchase.

The sale turned out to be Scotland's most popular of the century. An audience of over 500 crowded the sale ring at the

Ayr mart, with Kilpatrick and Dunlop standing stiff and
scowling on either side of the auctioneer.

The bidding opened at £3000. For a time it continued
between Dunlop and a breeder from Paisley. When £4000
was reached, however, Dunlop retired and, to the delight of
the sensation-hungry audience, Kilpatrick took over. The
bidding became brisker; but when it rose to £7000 the Paisley
breeder tore up his programme in despair and dropped out.

A stranger now appeared in the gallery and began bidding
against Kilpatrick. The audience held its breath. Dourly and
doggedly the price mounted until it seemed that the magic
and almost incredible figure of £10,000 might be reached.
But at £9500 Kilpatrick finally shook his head in angry
despair and the Baron was knocked down to the unknown
individual in the gallery.

Almost at once the denouement came, a blinding surprise
to some, half expected by others. While the ring was still
loud with excitement the auctioneer announced that the
stranger in the gallery had been bidding on behalf of William
Dunlop.

'Nine thousand five hundred pounds! Just imagine!' said
the old farmer who was relating the facts for my benefit. 'In
1911. What would be the equivalent today? Something like a
quarter of a million!' Then, the awe draining from his voice,
he added with a smile, 'The gauge of an Ayrshireman's
dourness!'

Three years later, in 1914, the Baron had to be destroyed
when a recalcitrant mare lashed out and broke one of his
forelegs. He was buried in the rose garden at Dunure Mains.
But his breeding prowess and the epic struggle between
Kilpatrick and Dunlop to possess him had aroused so much
international interest that in 1924 his skeleton was dug up,
reassembled and mounted in the Kelvingrove Art Galleries
in Glasgow, where this model of Clydesdale perfection may
still be seen.

It is pleasant to record that, in one way, the story had a
happy ending. In the early thirties some neighbours con-
spired to bring the two old enemies together at the Scotstoun
Stallion Show. By now they had mellowed: so much, indeed,

that they agreed to deliver a joint lecture at a meeting of
Clydesdale breeders at Milngavie. They called each other
'shrewd antagonists' and admitted that the price of the
Baron, both morally and materially, had been altogether too
high.

   They had tears in their eyes when the Baron was described
as 'that sensational and bewitching horse'.

There was nothing prim or prissy about the upbringing of a
country minister's son. Frequently he had to come to terms
with nature in what my mother liked to describe as its
'coarsest aspects'. But who can say this wasn't good for him?
Swear words, physical fights, torture (of and by others), sex
knowledge and sex jokes, all came within his experience at
an early age. On the other hand he was exposed daily to the
Christian teachings of his parents, so that his knowledge of
good and evil was provided in balance. Whether a proper
balance was acquired in my case – and in that of my four
brothers – must remain a matter of opinion.

   Sixty years ago a country minister's son could scarcely
avoid finding out that coarseness is not necessarily evil and
that fine professing Christians can be terrible hypocrites. A
minister's son today is able to discover this by watching
television, listening to the radio or reading the newspapers.
We had neither radio nor television; and only about half a
dozen copies of the *Glasgow Herald* came to the parish
before and during the First World War, to be shared among
the few, like my parents, who were interested in what was
going on outside Southend. (And who depended upon the
Herald's brilliant correspondent, Philip Gibbs, to present a
sane view of the international situation.) But I believe we
had an advantage over our modern counterparts. We were
involved not vicariously but at first hand in the rawness and
nobility of life.

   One piece of advice recurring in the Christian content of
our upbringing was a nut we found hard to swallow: 'Love
thy neighbour.' We could never summon up thoughts of love
in regard to Big Doser and Kleek. And when my father
roared and rampaged against members of his congregation

whom he judged to be sinners we wondered if he always practised what he preached.

My brothers and I, however, genuinely loved many of our neighbours. Mrs Galbraith at the shop, for example, who had a stammer and was inclined to shower with saliva the liquorice straps we bought with our pennies.

Everything to Mrs Galbraith was 'Tarrible, tarrible!' Pessimism concerning the weather, the government, attendances at church, the behaviour of her neighbours – and, in particular, our appetite for sweeties – were all condemned. But when we were sent for the messages she had an endearing habit, as we lifted the laden basket from the counter and prepared to leave, of picking large aniseed balls out of a jar and popping them into our mouths. (Experts on hygiene had not then begun to worry us. We belaboured one another with the liquorice straps and used aniseed balls for marbles, after which we ate them with unimpaired enjoyment.)

Then there was Mr Gutcher, the big, burly, heavily moustached lighthouse-keeper from the Mull, whose voice seemed to us to be as loud and resonant as the great mechanical horn he operated when fog lay thick across the North Channel. He was married to a prim, often silent little lady, deeply religious and dressed habitually in black, who, born in North Uist, was a distant relative of the Padre's. This blood connection, so important to the Gaels, was why they often came to tea at the Manse, which they used as a kind of staging post on their arduous shopping journey by horse and trap from the Mull to Campbeltown.

What his first name was I have no idea. We knew him simply as Mr Gutcher. Sixty years ago the habit of calling even casual acquaintances by their first names did not exist. Now, mature in years and striving to be with it, I am able to meet almost everybody on first-name terms, including ministers, lawyers, doctors, peers of the realm and many other people whose work and social position might seem to merit more unctuous respect. But there remains in my conscience a doubt as to the propriety of this, a legacy from the time when, as children, we were taught that age and learning and hereditary titles should be accorded full dignity. And yet it delights me that even the youngest child in Southend now calls me Angus. I should feel deprived of human contact if anybody addressed me as Mr MacVicar.

But in those more inhibited years it was Mr Gutcher. And Mrs Gutcher, even to my father, her cousin only a few stages removed.

What impressed me about Mr Gutcher was his knowledge of the many shipwrecks that had occurred at the Mull throughout the centuries. When his garden was out of season as a source of healthful exercise, he spent a great deal of his spare time in climbing along the rocky shores north and east of the lighthouse, searching for items cast up from broken and battered ships.

One day he brought two pistols to the Manse, both rusty and obviously no longer of practical use. One had been a lethal weapon, perhaps of American origin. The other was what I now know to have been a small gun for firing distress or other signals. To my delight and excitement he asked me to choose one to keep. The signal gun looked good: bigger and much more important looking than the other. So I chose it.

Next day, unknown to anyone in the Manse, I took it to school and had a satisfying time pointing it at Neil and other friends, threatening them with sudden death. Any girls whose curiosity brought them near were also threatened and made to run, screaming, from my powerful presence. I swaggered like a cowboy whose Indian enemies were biting the dust.

At last, of course, the inevitable happened. Some of the bigger boys, jealous of my newly acquired importance, ganged up to make an attack. They cornered me in the privvy and, as I struggled with my back against the wet, iron-lined wall of the urinal, wrenched the pistol out of my hot and slippery hands. Gallantly Neil tried to protect me; but they kicked him aside and ran out into the playground, shouting and fighting amongst themselves for possession of the prize.

In the midst of the commotion a whistle was blown with

loud authority. Into the playground strode Mr James Inglis Morton, the headmaster, his blond moustache bristling with anger. The bully boys dropped the pistol. I remember it lying there on the ash and gravel surface, silvery and sinister, while we all sucked in deep breaths of apprehension.

Mr Morton pointed. 'To whom does this belong?'

My nose was bleeding and the sleeve of my jersey was torn. I wanted to run away and hide; but there was no possible escape from Mr Morton's justice. I put up my hand.

He caught me by the ear. 'You have committed a crime of the most heinous nature,' he told me. 'Bringing a weapon to this school – it has never happened before in all its history. And,' he added, with terrible emphasis, 'it will never happen again as long as I am here!'

He paused. I was conscious that most of the girls had now gathered round, giggling. Anger began to dilute selfpity. Some of the boys who had attacked me, suddenly hopeful that I might be going to receive all the blame for the disturbance, were also smirking in the background. Tears of frustration mingled with the blood on my face. The taste of the mixture was bitter.

Then Mr Morton noticed my dishevelled appearance. 'Who did this to you?' he inquired.

Honour insisted that I remain silent. To be branded a 'clipe' (the Scots word for an informer) would be far worse than any physical scar. The same code kept other boys, including Neil, from telling the truth. But the girls had no such inhibitions.

'It was them!' they shouted, pointing at my attackers. 'They gi'ed him a moolkin in the privvy!' ('Moolkin' can be roughly translated as a 'beating up'.)

'Ah!' said Mr Morton, picking up the pistol while still retaining a grip of my ear. 'Come inside, all of you!'

The four boys who had taken the pistol were lined up alongside me in the empty classroom. Mr Morton took out his strap. Quietly and methodically he administered six of the best to each of us.

'I will now confiscate this horrible weapon,' he went on. 'During the next few days I will make up my mind whether or not to report the affair to the police.'

The sting of the belt soon passed and was as nothing, in terms of mental torture, compared with the menacing cloud of police action which now hung over us. I thought with horror of the shame which would come to my parents – innocents unaware of my criminality – if I were taken from the Manse in handcuffs and sent to prison. My assailants were in a similar state of fear. We became comrades in distress and full of friendship for one another. (Two of them are still alive. We remain friends.)

Of course, Mr Morton had no intention of bringing in the police. In time the menacing cloud disappeared below a clear horizon, and we essayed other forms of wickedness.

I never saw my signal pistol again. Years later, as an adolescent, I often played golf with Mr Morton, who was treasurer of our local club, Dunaverty. But my nerve always failed when I attempted to question him about it. He died a long time ago. I wonder what happened to it.

Mr Gutcher's pistol is a vivid memory. So is the story he told us about a Negro slave, the sole survivor from a Portuguese vessel wrecked in the eighteenth century underneath Borgadaile Cliff at the Mull. On his back he carried a small wooden barrel containing gold and jewels belonging to the master of the ship. He began climbing the cliff.

This is a dangerous business even in daylight. About twenty years ago, when a Peterhead fishing trawler ran aground at the same place, I was one of the rescue party which, as the tide rose, was forced to use the cliff as a way of egress from the shore. Scared almost to the point of paralysis, I could well imagine how the Negro must have felt in the gale-filled dark.

According to Mr Gutcher, however, he reached the top at last and made good his escape. But at some point in his climb he became so exhausted that he had to abandon the barrel and bury it deep in a crevice.

'The Negro,' said Mr Gutcher, as we listened with excitement, 'never returned to Southend. The treasure must still be there, in the cliff, waiting for some lucky boy to find it.'

That day as I climbed up from the stormy shore I

remembered the legend, but no longer did I feel an urge to search. I was only too thankful to reach the top. In any case, my eyes were closed most of the time.

Another of our favourites was old Mary MacAulay, who lived alone in a tiny 'but and ben' flat in the village and was often employed by my mother as a babysitter when she went with my father to Presbytery meetings in Campbeltown or – once a year – to the General Assembly in Edinburgh.

When sent to tell Mary that she was needed at the Manse, I always entered her flat with feelings of claustrophobia. The walls of her sitting-room were covered with several layers of paper. Above the small, deep-silled window the layers had curled upwards, like the bottom pages of a well-read manuscript, revealing plaster below. The room was crammed with cheap furniture, clocks and framed photographs. Being a clumsy boy, I kept barging into chairs and tables and tipping photographs from their precarious perches. But Mary never lost her cool. She restored the furniture and pictures to their original positions, patting my head and uttering giggles as she did so.

She was a small, round spinster of about sixty, enveloped from neck to toes in bulging garments. Her face was rosy and round. So was her mouth, which had a damp pout like the undersides of the limpets we sometimes gathered from the sea rocks. (My one fear of Mary was that she might try to kiss me. She never did.) In the village she was reputed by head-tapping wiseacres to be 'slightly ... you know!' On the other hand she loved children, calling them 'my wee dears', and her care of us at the Manse, when our parents and Mamie the maid were absent, was devoted and warm, even though her constant use of endearments was, to me at any rate, somewhat cloying.

It was her stories that I loved to hear. Sitting in the sun outside the Manse, sheltered from salty breezes by the rhododendron bushes, she would gather us round her like a hen with chickens and in her soft, slightly monotonous tone embark upon tales which were to us anything but monotonous.

A story we always asked for was about a fairy city which could sometimes be seen in the sea off the Mull of Kintyre. She made it real for us. In our imaginations we could picture without difficulty the tall buildings and the shimmering turrets that she described. On visits to the Mull we kept looking out beyond Fair Head in Ireland in case something might be visible in the great sweep of the Atlantic. We were always disappointed.

One day I asked her, 'When does this city appear?'

'Always in hot weather, dear, like the flowers in summer.'

'Have you seen it yourself, Mary?'

She looked sly. Glancing round to see if anyone but ourselves was listening, she whispered, 'Yes, I have seen it. On a day in August when I was gathering firewood on the shore. But this is a secret, mind. I don't want anyone else to know in case they think something is wrong with me.'

We wanted to believe that she had seen the fairy city. But I, for one, was content to appreciate the artistry of the story while remaining convinced that Mary was wandering and that the turrets and the sunlit streets that she described existed only in a fey corner of her mind.

Now I am not so sure.

The classical description of the Fata Morgana, the mirage of a magnificent city seen across the Straits of Messina, was published in 1773 by the Dominican friar, Antonio Minasi. (The name derives from Morgan le Fay, King Arthur's enchantress sister, whose magic could make a city appear on any shore in the world, luring seafarers to destruction and death.)

When the rising sun shines from that point whence its incident ray forms an angle of about 45 degrees on the sea of Reggio, and the bright surface of the water in the bay is not disturbed either by wind or the current, the spectator being placed on an eminence of the city, with his back to the sun and his face to the sea – on a sudden he sees appear in the water, as in a catoptric theatre, various multiple objects, such as numberless series of pilasters, arches, castles well delineated, regular columns, lofty towers, superb palaces with balconies and windows, extended alleys of trees, delightful plains with herds and flocks, armies of men on foot and horseback, and many other figures, all in their natural colours and proper action, and passing rapidly in succession along the surface of the sea, during the whole short period of time that the above-mentioned causes remain. But if, in addition to the circumstances before described, the atmosphere be highly impregnated with vapour and exhalations not dispersed by the wind nor rarefied by the sun, it then happens that in the vapour, as in a curtain extended along the channel to the height of about thirty palms and nearly down to the sea, the observer will behold the scene of the same objects not only reflected from the surface of the sea, but likewise in the air, though not in so distinct and defined a manner as in the sea. And again, if the air be slightly hazy and opaque, and at the same time dewy and adapted to form the iris, then the objects will appear only at the surface of the sea, but they will be all vividly coloured or fringed with red, green, blue and the other prismatic colours.

As I discovered during a wartime visit to the area, Minasi was born in Reggio in southern Italy. He saw the Fata Morgana three times. It is now accepted by scientists that his visions, in practical terms, were the refracted images of towns on the Sicilian coast (or, in one case, on the Calabrian coast), all remote from the place of observation. Since the time of Minasi, it seems that many people living in and around Reggio have witnessed the phenomenon.

At first, when reading about the Fata Morgana, I regarded it merely as a fable which might help me, as a writer, to illustrate how sin – and the sometimes beautiful face of sin – can lead the unwary to their souls' destruction. Because of its fabulous quality it aroused in me no memories of the tale told by Mary MacAulay about the city she had seen beyond the Mull, off the north coast of Ireland. Then, as in Reggio I encountered at first hand a popular belief in similar stories, a question stirred in my imagination.

After the Second World War, in an old copy of *Symons's Monthly Meteorological Magazine* for July 1871, I was surprised to find an anonymous article which indicated that the Fata Morgana might be pertinent to Scotland.

For some time past the atmospheric phenomena at the mouth of the Firth of Forth have been of a remarkably vivid and interesting character, and have attracted a great deal of attention. During the past week especially, scarcely a day has passed without exhibiting extraordinary optical illusions in connection with the surrounding scenery, both at sea and on shore.

As an instance of the unusual nature of these phenomena, the whole of the Broxmouth policies, mansion-house and plantation, were one day apparently removed out to sea.

One of the finest displays of mirage, however, occurred on Saturday afternoon. The early part of the day had been warm, and there was the usual dull, deceptive haze extending about half-way across the Forth, rendering the Fife coast invisible. The only object on the Fife coast, indeed, which was brought within the range of the refraction was Balconie Castle on the 'east neuk', which appeared half-way up the horizon, and in a line with the Isle of May.

The most extraordinary illusions, however, were those presented by the May island, which, from a mere speck on the water, suddenly shot up in the form of a huge perpendicular wall, apparently 800 or 900 feet high, with a smooth and unbroken front to the sea. On the east side lay a long low range of rocks, apparently detached from the island at various points, and it was on these that the most fantastic exhibitions took place.

Besides assuming the most diversified and fantastic shapes, the rocks were constantly changing their positions, now moving off, and again approaching each other. At one time a beautiful columnar circle, the column seemingly from 20 to 30 feet high, appeared on the outermost rock. Presently the figure was changed to a clump of trees, whose green umbrageous foilage had a very vivid appearance. By and by the clump of trees increased to a large plantation, which gradually approached the main portion of the island, until within 300 or 400 feet, when the intervening space was spanned by a beautiful arch. Another and another arch was afterwards formed in the same way, the spans being nearly of the same width, while the whole length of the island, from east to west, seemed as flat and smooth as the top of a table.

At a later period the phenomena, which were constantly chang-ing, showed huge jagged rifts and ravines in the face of the high wall, through which the light came and went as they opened and shut, while trees and towers, columns and arches sprang up and disappeared as if by magic.

It is a singular fact that during the four hours the mirage lasted, the lighthouse, usually the most prominent object from the south side of the Firth, was wholly invisible.

The last appearance which the island assumed was that of a thin blue line half-way up the horizon, with the lighthouse as a small pivot in the centre; and the extraordinary phantasmagoria were brought to a close about seven o'clock by a drenching rain, which fell for two hours.

Some time later I discovered a more recent Scottish connection: an article by D. Brent in a copy of *Nature* dated 17 February 1923.

The article described how, on the morning of 5 December 1922, at about 10.30 a.m., Mr John Anderson, lighthouse-keeper at the Cape Wrath Lighthouse, Durness, observed a strange mirage. He had focused his telescope on a conical hill about a quarter of a mile away (the height of the hill was approximately 200 feet) and was watching a sheep grazing there when suddenly he noticed something unusual in the surrounding atmosphere. He swung his telescope slightly upwards and saw a stretch of land and sea in the sky, at a height of about 1000 feet and in a southerly direction. Almost at once he recognized it as the coastline from Cape Wrath to Dunnet Head, as it might be seen from a ship ten miles out at sea.

Mr Anderson said that the mirage was visible only from a restricted area. At a distance of twenty yards on either side of the original position it could not be seen, though a movement of five yards from this point made no difference to the picture.

The mirage lasted for about half an hour. Then it was blotted out by heavy black clouds rearing up from the south-west. Rain began to fall, and during that afternoon the rain gauge at the lighthouse gave a total of 1.97 inches. The picture in the sky was seen by practically all the residents at the station.

All very factual and sensible. For me the Fata Morgana had become less of a fable, more a subject for scientific inquiry.

It seems, however, that scarcely any serious investigation by scientists has been carried out. In his book, *The Un-explained*, published in 1976, William R. Corliss writes:

Mirages sometimes display highly magnified objects. Islands and sites hundreds and even thousands of miles away may appear on the horizon. Polar ice may seem to be a distant mountain range; a fact which led to the embarrassing 'discovery' of Crockerland in the Arctic a few decades ago. Stones and hillocks became buildings and great mountains. To magnify in this fashion, the atmosphere must behave like a lens. Just how magnifying air lenses are formed is not well known.'

And then, finally, I came upon something which caused me not only surprise but also considerable excitement. It was contained in the *History of the Parish of Ramoan (Ballycastle)*, by the Rev. William Connolly, published in 1812.

The Rev. William, it appears, had received 'a minute description of the Fata Morgana from several persons who saw it, on different summer evenings, along the shore of the Giant's Causeway.' Castles, ruins and tall spires had appeared on the surface of the sea, sometimes expanding to considerable heights. He had been told also that a man who lived near the causeway had seen an 'enchanted' island 'floating' along the coast of Antrim.

From Irish friends I have now discovered that stories about the Fata Morgana – such as that, for example, concerning the green island that every seventh year rises from the sea off Rathlin Island, opposite Ballycastle – are common in Ulster. In fact, specific instances have been recorded by that august body, the British Association. What appeared to be a city, with its streets, its houses and its spires, was seen in 1817 over the Ferry at Lough Foyle. A similar mirage appeared close to the Bannmouth on 14 December 1850.

The legendary references to Rathlin and the Giant's Causeway are for me particularly significant. We can see them both clearly from the Mull of Kintyre, a dozen miles away across the North Channel. And it was in this area, out at sea, that old Mary MacAulay said she had seen a 'fairy city'.

Was she so wandered after all?

Perhaps some day, if I am lucky, I will stand among the heather high above the Mull and see, on the horizon beyond the Giant's Causeway, the fantastic city that was her secret pride.

And secret fear.

I suppose that the Fata Morgana, in a metaphorical sense, occurs frequently in all our lives. Like James Kilpatrick and William Dunlop, like Mr Gutcher and old Mary MacAulay, like the Negro slave with his barrel of jewels, we catch a glimpse of beauty and romance and, when the vision fades, experience secret disappointment.

But sometimes the vision becomes real. It is then we have an intimation of the meaning of divine love. Instead of an ideal seen through a glass darkly we come, for a moment, face to face with it; and our courage is renewed.

5. A Boy in Uist

Long before I was born there had been another boy.

One day he sat cross-legged on a flat stone in a cleft of the rocks: rocks which sheltered him from a snell east wind. In his hand was a rusty, blunt knife with which he was shaping, in labour and frowning difficulty, a plank of wood he had found on the strand below him.

His hair was plentiful and Viking fair, his face, red with exertion, spotted with freckles. His feet were bare, the soles dirty and leather-hard. He wore a woollen jersey and a pair of carefully patched trousers. The jersey had been knitted by his mother with wool garnered from the family sheep and spun on her clacking wheel. She had also fashioned the trousers from sturdy cloth made with the same wool on an island loom.

The year was 1889. It was Sunday, and he was eleven years old.

Across the sound, a late spring sun was dipping above the islands which lay between the flat shore of North Uist and the Atlantic. Banks of yellow and purple faded down the sky, squeezing the sun rays into brilliant laser beams. As the beams moved they caused tiny explosions of light to occur on the sea and on the piles of wet dulse and tangle at the sea's edge. Congregations of black oystercatchers, which the boy knew as *gille bride* (the servants of St Bride), strutted on stiff red legs, sometimes on the wet sand, sometimes in the slow curl of the wavelets. They complained harshly when seagulls, careless on evening joy flights, strayed into their feeding grounds.

From the little township on the machair land above and behind the rock cleft there came an aromatic drift of peat smoke. It overwhelmed the acrid scents of young vegetation from the low hills in the island's interior and the salt scents from the shore. The boy's concentration was broken. Burgeoning peat smoke meant that his mother was cooking the daily supper of maizemeal porridge, and it came to him with a small shock that it was long past the time when he ought to have been home.

He shivered. His work with the knife was only half done, but he would have to leave it, for the time being at any rate. It would grieve his mother that he had stayed out so late, especially on a Sunday, and he had no wish to add to her grief. What excuse could he make to her? One thing was sure: he could never say that he had become so absorbed in the making of a shinty stick – he called it a *caman* – that he had forgotten the passage of time. Cutting a *caman* on a Sunday.... Dark fears invaded his brain. Precursors of the pains of Hell?

Within the cleft a narrow crevice burrowed farther into the rocks. Into this he pushed the hacked wood and the knife. He hoped nobody would look into the crevice until he could retrieve them tomorrow after school. New apprehension came to him as he remembered this was a place his grandfather often visited to say his prayers. Then apprehension faded. His grandfather was ninety-four and blind. There was no real danger.

He emerged from the cleft into the east wind, which blew cold across the flat, treeless land of North Uist from the mountains of Ross and Inverness-shire beyond the Minch. By this time dusk was falling, and he could see a blink from the Monach lighthouse, far to the west. His cousin Donald, who was five years older, had once told him that if he looked through a linen handkerchief he could see the slats in the lighthouse windows. His parents being too poor to afford linen handkerchiefs, he had never been able to make the experiment. He suspected that his cousin was making a joke at the expense of his ignorance, but he wasn't quite sure. He had been brought up to believe so many strange stories, both sacred and secular, that at the age of eleven he wasn't sure of anything. Except, perhaps, of one thing: he needed that

caman to show the other boys – and especially his cousin
Donald – that he was as strong and as good at playing shinty
as they were. If not stronger and better.

He was met by his mother at the back door of the
crofthouse. She spoke – and he answered – in the Gaelic.

'Where have you been, Angus John?'

'On the shore.'

'On a Sunday? Until this time of night?'

'I'm sorry, mother.'

'What were you doing?'

He said nothing. He couldn't lie to her.

'Were you with the other boys?'

'Yes. But they went home a long time ago.'

She asked no more questions.

Seventy years later Angus John was to tell us, 'While my
mother washed my feet preparatory to my going to bed, she
lectured me about what, according to the Book, would
happen at the last to bad boys who broke the Sabbath. That
night, I remember, I fell asleep with a sore heart, sobbing
bitterly, not because I had possibly displeased God but
because I had hurt my mother's feelings.'

And he found little comfort in the knowledge that he
would have hurt them a great deal more had he confessed
he'd been using a knife to make a *caman*. His father had
forbidden him to carry a knife, because of the danger to
himself and to other people. To use one on a Sunday was
surely a terrible sin. Made even more terrible, perhaps,
because he was keeping it a secret.

In the event, like all sins, it did not remain a secret for
long. While his mother was washing his feet, Angus John
noticed that his grandfather was absent from his usual chair
in the dark, smoky kitchen. Supping porridge with a horn
spoon, his father explained, 'When he heard you coming in
he went out, down to the shore, to say his prayers.' Another
tremor of apprehension troubled Angus John; but it was
soon forgotten in his sorrow at having made his mother
unhappy.

Next day, carrying his peat for the classroom fire (a daily
duty for all the children), he went to the Claddach Kirkibost

school, which had been built in 1883 only a few hundred yards down the road from his parents' croft. With sixty others he began the day by repeating the Lord's Prayer, in English, and answering a few questions from the Shorter Catechism. Then he settled down to the tedious and painful process of learning to read and write and do simple arithmetic. His teacher, a girl from Elgin, spoke no Gaelic. Not until he was five years old had he himself learned to speak English, and his brain still worked in the Gaelic. Frustration resulted, for both of them.

Coming home from school in the afternoon, Angus John took a roundabout route, by way of the shore. When he reached the cleft in the rocks he found, to his acute discouragement, that his grandfather was sitting on a nearby boulder. The old man's chin rested on the horn handle of his *cromack*. His blind eyes stared out towards the sea. But he heard – and recognized – the footsteps on the shingle.

'There you are, Angus John, I have been waiting for you.'

'It's getting cold, grandfather. Don't you think you ought to be going back inby?'

'In a minute, in a minute. Last night I found some interesting things in that crevice in there.'

Angus John felt as if he might choke. What awful punishment was this old man – so venerable, so severely upright in all his ways according to the stories – about to bring down on him? He swallowed a spittle and did not speak.

'A knife, Angus John, and a piece of wood.'

Would his grandfather tell his parents? Or would he, here and now, utter some curse against sinning boys: some cruel curse dredged up from the pagan lore of the island? Still he remained silent.

Then, in wheezing weakness, like a fading thunderstorm, the old man began to chuckle. 'Whoever is trying to make a *caman* out of that stick is making a terrible bad job of it!'

To share the secret, whatever the consequences might be, brought relief. And release.

'It's a terrible bad knife, grandfather. I found it on the rubbish heap.'

'A lambing knife that I once used myself, fifty years ago. I kept it in the byre. Your father threw it away when it got rusty.' He held out his hand. 'Come here, *laochain*.'

Angus John hesitated.

'Don't be afraid. I'll not be telling a soul.'

Angus John moved forward and found his hand gripped by the gnarled old one. 'You're a bad boy, of course,' said his grandfather. 'But all boys are bad. I was bad myself at your age. Do you know, Angus John, we used to *play* shinty on a Sunday!'

'On a *Sunday*, grandfather?'

'Ay. Before the morning service. And we would be running and jumping, too. And putting the stone.'

'*Chiall!* Did you not get into terrible rows?'

'Ach, we did so, especially from the minister if he caught us at it. But everybody was doing it, so we didn't mind the rows so much.' He sighed. 'Nowadays, everything is so stern and black, there's no joy in it.'

'I can see what you mean, grandfather.'

'Jesus Christ died to make us happy. If we find no joy in living, is it not unfair to Him?'

They listened to the small waves hissing on the sand. After a while the old man said, 'Are you keen on the shinty?'

Angus John's astonishment at his grandfather's revelations was replaced by enthusiasm. 'Desperate keen,' he said. 'Cousin Donald says I'm no good, but if I had a real *caman* I would show him!'

'Ay, so you would. But by the feel of it you'll never make a decent *caman* out of that old plank. Listen. Do you know Roderick MacAulay over at Claddach?'

'Ay, Gillesbuig's father. Gillesbuig and I are in the same class.'

'Well, go and see Roderick. In his day he was a great man at making *camans*, and he still has a few left. Tell him I sent you to get one.'

'Oh, grandfather ... '

'Now I must be going back to the house. Your mother will be wondering what on earth I'm doing.'

That night Angus John went to sleep in a mood completely different from that of the night before. His thoughts were happy and excited. Liberated, too. The grandfather he had always looked upon as a kind of brooding Jehovah was, after all, a human being like himself. Perhaps the grown-up people in North Uist – like his father and mother, for example – weren't all as good and holy as they made themselves out to be. Perhaps life wouldn't prove to be the unhappy burden they so often sighed and groaned about. And now, now there would be a real shinty stick to play with.

Years later Angus John wrote about his grandfather with love and regard. But he didn't put the story I have just told into print: that was given to his sons in private when he considered them mature enough to understand. Instead, as an outwardly staid old minister, approaching the age of ninety, he published the following:

My grandfather chose a place for private prayer between two slabs of rock on the shore below the croft house. Sometimes on a Sunday evening, and always at times of sorrow and distress, he would kneel there on a flat stone in the cleft of the rocks, facing the east with clasped hands, making his requests known to God and seeking forgiveness, mercy and help. In my memory's eye I can still see him, returning to the house from his place of prayer, bent and blind, wearing a Highland bonnet and with a staff in his hand. Was his choice of that 'Stony Bethel' something he had inherited from his ancestors, the priests?

Fine resounding stuff, appropriate to a man who had preached from the pulpit of St Blaan's at the Mull of Kintyre almost every Sunday for forty-seven years. He meant it, I believe, to be an example of holy living for the benefit of his congregation and his less than holy family.

But there was more to the Rev. Angus John MacVicar, MA, JP, than the ability to sermonize. I ought to know. He was my father.

In the summer of 1920, at the age of eleven and a bit, I went to North Uist with my father. It was a long journey.

First, a horse-drawn bus conveyed us from Southend to Campbeltown, where we boarded the steamer *Kinloch* for Gourock.

As the *Kinloch* ploughed an elegant passage through Kilbrannan Sound we breakfasted on ham and eggs, warm barm biscuits and strong tea. Spreading marmalade on a third barm biscuit, I thought I had never tasted anything so good. Oily smells from the throbbing engine room mingled with a fresh saltiness gusting down the companionway from a spray-damp deck. The steamer plunged among short and shallow waves. Some passengers, cocooned in rugs, lay prone and silent on the saloon benches. My father said they were seasick. My sorrow for their condition soon faded, and I would have tackled a fourth barm biscuit had there been any left.

At Gourock we took a train to Glasgow. There, at his flat in Berkeley Street, we stayed for a night with yet another Angus MacVicar, a retired detective sergeant who was my father's second cousin.

Early the following morning we caught a train for Mallaig, and as the sun rose above the smoke-grey mountains of Argyll which came towering up on either side of us, I was filled with excitement. This was the life. Surely, around every corner of the track, there must lurk astounding adventure and romance: explosions, an attack by Red Indians, a pride of lions which had escaped from a zoo. When adventure and romance failed to materialize (though it did occur in my imagination), I was only vaguely disappointed.

During the Second World War, journeying with my battalion in varying degrees of discomfort through Madagascar, India, Persia, Palestine, Sicily, Italy, France, Belgium and Germany, I often experienced the same sense of excited anticipation. In the final count, however, it was my eventual return home to Southend which provided me with the only real and lasting satisfaction.

I think most Celts have this kind of nature: we love to travel and taste adventure; but what we love most is home and the comfort of friendly neighbours. Few of us are bred to endure the hard and lonely lives of emperors and kings. Like his forebears who saw visions and lit up our dangerous coasts, Robert Louis Stevenson was a Celt. In his *El Dorado* (a title which, in a sense, may be translated as Fata

Morgana) he wrote: 'To travel hopefully is a better thing
than to arrive, and the true success is to labour.'

At Mallaig my father and I took the steamer *Sheila* for
Lochmaddy. Her skipper, in the Gaelic, hailed the Padre as a
long-lost friend. We were taken to his cabin, where I felt
some constraint as they talked, with much laughter and a
succession of drams, in a language that wasn't mine.

I didn't know it then, but this stout, benign, whiskery
character was to become a legend amongst travellers to the
Hebrides. Stories about him are still bandied about in the
saloon bars of many little steamers plying the island seas
from Ullapool and Stornoway to Port Ellen and Tarbert.

It seems that when he spoke in English he always pronounced 'th' as 's', a common habit of the Gaels. Once, in the
Kyles of Lochalsh, he was hailed by the owner of a small
yacht, an anxious Englishman, who, when asked if something
was wrong, shouted up at him, 'I'm sinking, skipper! I'm
sinking!' To which, leaning comfortably on the bridge, the
skipper replied, 'Well, well, and what are you sinking
about?'

Another tale told of him is worth repeating. It concerns a
North Uist girl setting out for Glasgow, where she hoped to
enter domestic service. Halfway across the Minch in the
Sheila she was asked to show her ticket. As she fumbled for it
in her handbag, a testimonial to her character supplied by
her local minister was snatched away by the gusty wind. She
began to cry, believing that she might miss the chance of
securing work if she were unable to produce a reference. But
the redoubtable skipper was equal to the occasion. 'Never
you mind, lassie,' he said. 'I'll give you a certificate that will
see you through.' And there and then he sat down and wrote
it: 'This is to certify that on the night of the seventh
November in the Minch, on board the SS *Sheila*, Kirsty
MacLean lost her character.'

That day in the *Sheila*, however, as my father and I crossed
to Lochmaddy, I was kept in ignorance of such Gaelic
delights. In fact, I was bored. And even more bored,
perhaps, when we left the skipper's cabin and went on deck,
where my father spoke to several of the crew, again in the

Gaelic. He told me that most of them came from North Uist and were related to the MacVicars. He found pleasure in their company. I didn't. Communication between me and them appeared to be impossible.

Later on, in North Uist, while my father and I holidayed with my grandparents in their old 'black house' at Claddach Kirkibost, I began to get the proper feel of the island.

I went about barefoot. On the shore I found the two slabs of rock with the cleft between them which, according to the Padre, my great-grandfather had used as a place of prayer. (He didn't tell me then about the knife and the half-finished *caman* he himself had hidden in the cleft.)

I visited my cousins, the MacAulay boys, at their family farm of Balelone. Roderick and Angus were both slightly older than I was and, even by the standards set by Big Doser and Kleek, fairly hard men, tough and rough. They had a big *garron* (a small island-bred horse) which they said I must ride bareback. Apprehensively, I allowed them to give me a leg up. As I sat clutching the beast's mane and trying to achieve a balance on her broad but slippery back, they struck her on the rump with a stick. She took off like a demented thing, rearing and squirming, and I was flung high into the air. I landed on the ground head first. Luckily the ground consisted of peat moss covered with scraggy heather, and the only lasting injury was to my self-esteem. But it shook me a little to observe that the dent I had made in the turf was only a few inches away from a large boulder.

That evening, at dusk, Roderick and Angus played the same joke on me – so I learned years later – as my father's cousin Donald had tried to play on him. They told me to look through my linen handkerchief at the Monach light in the distance. 'Can't you see them,' they said, 'the slats in the lighthouse windows?' Still suffering both morally and physically from my fall, I was in no mood to offer a polite reply. I remembered crude words used by old Charlie in Southend and addressed them, with some vehemence, to my cousins. They laughed, but from that time they treated me more as an equal.

I loved the days with Roderick and Angus, helping to

gather sheep for clipping, working with them in the hayfields and coming home to supper at the farmhouse, at which, on one occasion, a dish of skate was served and I was astonished by the way my Uncle Roderick – big, blond and hearty – crunched through all the gristly bones and swallowed them along with the rest of the fish.

But even more I loved the summer evenings at my grandparents' 'black house', when they and my father and I would sit outside in the quiet, tangle-scented air, while neighbours (most of them close relatives and all of them male) gathered to talk.

At first I had difficulty in teasing out the relationships between all the Anguses, Donalds, Gillesbuigs and Rodericks who took part in those *ceilidhs*. There were (translated from the Gaelic) Big Anguses and Wee Anguses, Black Donalds and Fair Donalds, Frowning Gillesbuigs and Smiling Gillesbuigs, Balelone Rodericks and Claddach Rodericks, Balelone and Claddach being the names of the farms or crofts occupied by the individuals concerned. In addition, there were Donald Gillesbuigs and Gillesbuig Donalds, Roderick Anguses and Angus Rodericks. (Among my female cousins I had already found in the same family a Mary Maggie and a Maggie Mary.) After a time I began to realize that behind it all there lay a steady logic, based on custom, and soon – after about the third or fourth *ceilidh* – I was able to judge the degree of consanguinity almost at the drop of a name.

In most Hebridean families, including my own, there is an unwritten law which dictates that the eldest son should be called after his grandfather on the father's side and the eldest daughter after the grandmother on the mother's side. The second son is called after the maternal grandfather and the second daughter after the paternal grandmother. Other children inherit their names from great-uncles or great-aunts in strict order of seniority. Maggie Marys and Mary Maggies occur in the same family when the appropriate great-aunts happen to have the same name. Then *their* mothers' names are taken into account.

One boy I met in North Uist answered to the unusual

name of Nappy Neil. At one of the *ceilidhs* I learned that this
was because of an unfortunate hiccup, some generations
back, in the age-old custom. A young crofter and his wife had
been arguing about a name for their newborn second son.
The young crofter's father was Neil, so, of course, they
already had a son who had been christened Neil. As misfor-
tune would have it, the maternal grandfather was also Neil.
The young crofter wanted his wife to waive her father's right
and choose another name: but the mother was adamant. 'We
will call him Neil, Donald. But if you like we can put another
name before it, just to make a difference.' It was about this
other name that the argument continued to rage.

The day came when the young father had to register the
child's birth, and, as he prepared to go, no solution to the
disagreement had been reached. He was about to slam his
way outside when his wife, highly incensed, shouted after
him, 'Och, have it your own way! Call him what you like!
Call him Napoleon if it suits you!' In his highly charged state
of mind Donald took her at her word. The little boy's name
was registered as Napoleon Neil. And, because the old
custom was never again tampered with, there are a number
of boys in the Hebrides, even to this day, known as Nappy
Neil.

Another story which I thought was funny – amongst others
concerned with superstitions, most of them sad and inexplic-
able – concerned a *bodach* (elderly man) in Claddach
Kirkibost who was going home one night in the dark and
heard behind him the slide and slither of footsteps. He began
to run. The footsteps quickened, too. Courageously he
slowed down again. The footsteps slowed as well. At last,
panic-stricken, he took full flight and eventually irrupted into
the house, where his wife was preparing supper. 'Kirsteen,
Kirsteen,' he panted, 'the hounds of hell are after me!' She
looked down at his right foot. 'It's a funny kind of hound,'
she said, calmly, pointing to a length of straw, caught in the
heel plate of his boot, which had been trailing behind him.

Those evening *ceilidhs* at my grandfather's house were
generally conducted in the Gaelic; but sometimes, for my
benefit, my father or grandfather would translate the stories,

especially if they concerned our ancestors in the island. Gradually, even though in a boyish blur, I became aware that I was acquiring lessons in heredity. The blood of those ancient people of North Uist ran in my veins. Their physical characteristics and modes of conduct were my heritage. Their triumphs and tragedies might well come to be echoed in my own future.

It intrigued me how all my relatives spoke about our forebears in a detached kind of way, as if they were referring to some family in which they had no personal interest. The MacVicars, they told me, while 'short in the grain' (a Scots phrase meaning quick-tempered but originally descriptive of brittle wood), had a reputation for generosity. They were also foolish so far as money was concerned. According to legend, they were deeply religious, though it appeared that some, including my great-grandfather, had eyes for the girls, and I deduced that in spite of our aspirations to holiness we had more blood relatives in the Hebrides than those born with the same name.

Each night, when the *ceilidh* was over, the four of us would go indoors, where, by the light of a paraffin lamp, my father would conduct family worship.

My grandfather was a middle-aged, round, choleric man, with the greying remnants of a blond beard. My grand-mother was slim and quiet and dark, with a look in her eyes which I could not – and still cannot – explain. It might have been one of shyness. Or perhaps, more likely, of suffering. It struck me, however, as gentle, threatening nobody.

Sadness appeared to be the background to all their religious exercises. As my father prayed or read from the Bible they would groan and sigh and shake lowered heads. This was such a contrast to my grandfather's robust behaviour at other times that, even then, I was inclined to wonder if the whole performance might be tainted a little by hypocrisy. The meekness and sad resignation with which my grandfather listened to the Word were completely out of tune, in my opinion, with his voluble rage, punctuated by terrible Gaelic oaths, when I failed to do his bidding and turn a group of frisky young cattle from the roadway into a field.

I remember how bitterly I resented being made the target for his anger. I left him to deal with the cattle himself and went into the house to sit, sulking, with my grandmother. Patiently, while stirring a big iron pot hanging from a soot-encrusted chain above the fire, she posed question after question until at last I blurted out the truth of what had happened. Then she smiled and said, 'Ah, *laochain*, you're a real MacVicar!' She herself was a MacLean of Boreray (an island district in North Uist), the daughter of a family which claimed ancient kinship with the Lords of the Isles. Perhaps that was why she was able to understand and forgive the petty tantrums of the less aristocratic MacVicars.

As we sat there talking, my grandmother and I, my bruised feelings were almost forgotten; and what I now remember most vividly about that day was the evening meal she gave us. It consisted of flounders and new potatoes boiled together in sea water in the big pot, followed by a dish of *carageen* and cream. (*Carageen* is a kind of blancmange, the main ingredient of which is powdered dulse, a variety of seaweed found plentifully on Hebridean coasts.)

I have never tasted a meal more appetizing. They tell me that my enjoyment of it resulted from the fact that I was young and healthy at the time. I believe this argument to be specious. It resulted from the fact that the fish had been taken straight from the sea, that the potatoes had been grown on the croft without artificial aid, seawrack from the nearby shore being the only fertilizing agent, that the *carageen* was homemade and the cream taken from the tiny dairy at the back of the house: nothing packed in tin or plastic to make its flavour flat, nothing with all taste processed and frozen out of it. I feel sorry for most young people today, especially for those born and brought up in an urban environment. They just don't know how delicious natural food can be. Even though old, I still have a healthy appetite and can tell immediately the awful difference between a sweet and tender chicken, reared naturally out of doors, and a battery-produced monstrosity, frozen and packed in plastic and tasting like slimy rubber.

My grandfather and grandmother, though groaning and

sighing whenever the name of Christ was mentioned, still gave thanks to God continually for His material mercies. They invoked His blessing at all times – before meals, before milking the cows, before clipping the sheep, before setting out for a night's fishing. Those observances struck me as being basically different from the Sabbath-orientated religion generally practised on the mainland.

The people of North Uist acknowledged their dependence on God on all occasions, secular as well as sacred: ostensibly, at any rate. It was only long afterwards that I came to understand that they were carrying out the practices of the old Celtic Church founded in Scotland by St Columba: practices which implied that religion was bound up with everyday things and could not be divorced from 'ploughing and sowing and reaping and mowing' and which, indeed, endorsed the Druidical belief that to identify with nature was also to identify with God.

But it seemed to me, though still only a boy, that such practices, as carried out by my grandparents, had become little more than superstition: a kind of lip service to religion, which decreed groans and sighs at the thought of the death of Christ rather than shouts of joy, as was His will. St Columba and his disciples had made the original Celtic Church a happy band of brothers. This latter-day version was a pale imitation, partially drained of vitality, though still containing traces of wry humour.

An example of this humour is contained in a story I heard my grandfather tell, accompanied by quiet chuckles in his beard. It concerned a middle-aged cousin of his in North Uist who, for years, on Tuesday and Saturday nights, travelled on foot a distance of almost ten miles to see his girl. One day a friend took Donald to task. 'Donald,' he said, 'you're not getting any younger, and here you are, year after year, every Tuesday and Saturday, walking all those miles to see Morag. Why don't you make up your mind to marry her?' 'Well,' said Donald, 'it's true what you say about me getting older. But if I married her, what on earth would I do for recreation?'

But such happy stories were rare in comparison with the

sad and unhappy ones. How had all this pessimism and lack of vitality come about? The question lay in a corner of my mind for years, existing in parallel with a growing interest in the people and the environment which had produced my father. During our time in North Uist he took me to see many places and many people. About them he told me an abundance of tales and legends which I put aside in quiet storage for a time when I might be faced with trying to explain, in part at any rate, the kind of man he was.

This time has now come. And it occurs to me that if by engaging in such an exercise I can find clues to his character, then, by the laws of heredity, I may find some to my own.

When I stayed in it on holiday in 1920, my grandparents' 'black house', thatched with heather, had few comforts. It had still fewer, about a hundred years ago, when the Padre was a boy.

At that time it was like every other crofter's house in North Uist, a long narrow building with the kitchen and bedroom at one end and the barn and the byre at the other. The windows were glazed slits in the stone walls. The kitchen had an earthen floor, and the smoke's main exit was a hole in the roof. Under the kitchen window a wooden bench flanked a box for the peat. Along the opposite wall there stood a dresser and a row of chests containing the family's Sunday clothes. In the other room – the only other room – were two wooden beds. The bedding consisted of clean straw or dried bent grass, which, my father told me, was changed twice a year in June and November. Light on dark evenings, when neighbours would call, was provided by a *cruiskan*, a small dish of oil with a wick in it, which usually stood on the dresser. The oil was rendered down from the flesh of seals and, at times, from that of small whales found stranded on the beaches.

Living conditions were not much better than in some parts of tribal Africa. The only education my father's parents ever received was in the church schools, where they were taught to read the Bible and the Shorter Catechism in Gaelic.

The family croft was small, as it still was in 1920, with only a few acres of pasture; and yet, lacking either grants or subsidies, my grandfather, Angus MacVicar, persevered in his own limited way and struggled to augment his meagre income by working also as a dealer. At the beginning of summer he usually bought some young cattle, grazed them on the nearby tidal islands of Baleshare or Illeray and then sold them at the autumn markets. Every August he sold his season's lambs to the more prosperous Lewis and Harris men who came looking for bargains. At the end of September he often bought old ewes from the crofters of comparatively distant Locheport and Grimsay and sold them to his neighbours, sometimes having to wait for his money for years. As a standing order, he dispatched fifty ewes annually to a farmer in Tiree.

My grandmother, whose maiden name was Isabella Mac-Lean, was no less industrious. In the kitchen, which was her province, with its damp floor and smoky atmosphere, she cooked and washed with water from the township's common well, pedalled her spinning wheel, sewed and knitted and fashioned clothes for her son and daughter and, in winter, tended the cattle chewing and steaming at the other end of the building.

Such unremitting labour, however, did not bring many physical advantages to the children. Indian meal porridge was my father's staple diet, and only occasionally did he savour the luxury of a mutton stew or a dish of salt herrings and potatoes. From April to October he ran about barefoot. Even on a day when wind and rain swept over the comfortless flats of North Uist he had to do without an overcoat when he visited the toilet, which was the open machair.

In this primitive environment, with its cultural and material poverty, the old people of North Uist, like the MacVicars, retained a kind of dignity: a dignity supported by a long tradition of religious belief and of family history handed down by word of mouth from generation to generation. My father, however, even in his young days, recognized it as having become sad and submissive, enfeebled by a fatalism which probably stemmed from the Clearances which had occurred some fifty years before, at a time when men,

women and children were herded aside to make way for
sheep and when it seemed that nobody cared, neither lairds
nor ministers nor government officials. There was a stirring
in his head of rebellion, of a desire to throw aside the
blankets of poverty, superstition and inertia under which his
people cowered.

But the North Uist folk had seen happier and more
prosperous times. They used them as pegs on which to hang
their pride.

6. Son of the Vicar

My father was always proud of his family history, the focus of such pride being Trinity Temple (Teampull na Trionaid) in Carinish, which lies in the moorland some four or five miles south-east of Claddach Kirkibost.

As he told me on our day-long pilgrimage to its ancient ruins, Trinity Temple is one of the oldest ecclesiastical buildings in the Outer Hebrides and, next to Roidil (St Clement's) in Harris, the most important. It was founded in 1263, on the site of an old Columban dedication, by Belliag, the first Prioress of Iona, who was a daughter of Somerled, the great ancestor of the MacDonalds. It was rebuilt and repaired in the middle of the fourteenth century by Amie NicRhuari, the discarded wife of John of Islay (who called himself the first Lord of the Isles), and reconstructed in its present form during the sixteenth century. Measuring 61 feet 8 inches by 21 feet 6 inches, its walls average in thickness about 40 inches.

Never a place of public worship, except on special occasions such as Christmas and Easter, it functioned principally as a college of learning, where, according to the Clan Donald historians, young men of the Isles were trained for the priesthood. Though reckoned to be older than such highly acclaimed religious schools as those at Ardchattan, Lismore and Saddell in Kintyre, it was never so well endowed or so influential in its teaching. It had connections, however, with the Augustinian Abbey of Inchaffray in Maderty, Perthshire, and with the collegiate church of Kilmun on the shores of the Holy Loch in Cowal, Argyll.

Tradition has it that the progenitor of the North Uist MacVicars was born in Argyll and, in the late thirteenth

century, went from the collegiate church of Kilmun as a
teacher priest, in much the same way as a modern lecturer in
Divinity at Glasgow University might move to Edinburgh on
being appointed professor there. As priests of the medieval
Celtic Church were untrammelled by vows of celibacy, he
was probably succeeded in this hereditary office by his son
(or sons), because, during the following centuries, MacVicars
are recorded on the ecclesiastical and civil scene of the island
as teachers and priests and also as editors and custodians of
documents belonging to the Church and to the Lords of the
Isles.

An act of parliament, dated 13 June 1496, ordered that 'all
barons and freeholders who are of substance send their
eldest sons and heirs from eight or nine years of age to the
schools and remain there until they become completely
educated and have perfect Latin, and thereafter remain
three years at the Schools of Art and Law so that they may
have knowledge and understanding of the laws.' The penalty
for non-compliance was a salutary fine of twenty pounds
Scots. There is no doubt that Trinity Temple and its associated schools came under the terms of this act.

According to my father, the first MacVicar of more than
local importance appeared in the fifteenth century: Domh-
nuill Mac an Abba (Donald, son of the Abbot). Himself
probably a lay abbot, he is said to have been a man of
influence in both church and state affairs.

Alexander, Lord of the Isles (a grandson of John of Islay),
cherished an ambition to bring Orkney and Shetland under
his Gaelic rule. With the approval of the king, therefore, he
organized an expedition from the Islands to Inverness,
Easter Ross and Sutherland, its purpose being to persuade
men in those areas to join him in a seaborne invasion of the
Northern Isles. The 'public relations officers' attached to the
expedition included an Irish orator, an Irish diplomat and
Donald MacVicar.

Their propaganda had little effect. The people of the
northern mainland turned their backs on Lord Alexander,
obviously preferring a peaceful if poor existence to the
danger inherent in yet another MacDonald adventure. It

appears that Donald failed in his advocacy, as did many a MacVicar who came after him.

It has often occurred to me to wonder how a lay abbot such as Donald would be dressed. My father, whose knowledge of the olden days in North Uist depended in the main upon information supplied by the *sennachies* (storytellers), was vague about this detail. Recently, however, on rereading Martin Martin's *A Description of the Western Islands of Scotland*, first published in 1695, I discovered a passage which may be relevant.

Referring to a lay monk with whom he spoke in Benbecula, Martin wrote that this *brahir-brocht* (poor brother) had nothing but what was given him.

He holds himself fully satisfied with food and raiment, and lives in great simplicity. His diet is mean and he drinks only fair water. His habit is no less mortifying than that of his brethren elsewhere. He wears a short coat, which comes no further than his middle, with narrow sleeves like a waistcoat. He wears a plaid above it, girt about the middle, which reaches to his knee. The plaid is fastened on his breast with a wooden pin, his neck bare, and his feet often so, too. He wears a hat for ornament, and the string about it is a bit of fishing line made of horse hair. This plaid he wears instead of a gown worn by lay monks in other countries. I told him he wanted the flaxen girdle that men of his order usually wear. He answered me that he wears a leather one, which was the same thing. This poor man lies upon straw. He frequently diverts himself with the angling of trouts.

I'm glad I'm not a lay abbot like some of my ancestors. The only part of their existence which might appeal to me is that they could engage in 'the angling of trouts'.

It seems that another MacVicar – another Donald, indeed – held an important though perhaps somewhat unenviable position under the Lords of the Isles. On several of their expeditions from the Hebrides to the mainland, most of them still aimed at the annexation of Orkney and Shetland, he acted as a kind of quartermaster general, responsible for the troops' food and equipment. On the transport side his worries must have been severe, with only small, insubstantial craft at his disposal to ferry fighting men across the stormy Minches.

None of the raids proved successful. This second Donald, like the first, found himself on the losing side.

A song (or part of a song) relating to one of those raids (in 1460) still lives among the islanders. I remember, vaguely, hearing it sung in the Gaelic by an old lady in Claddach Kirkibost, who had no teeth and wore a mutch (cap). The English translation begins:

> Our expedition did not have bloodshed in view,
> Our object was the cementing of friendship.
> In the land of clouds, kyles and cold winds
> They had the choice of Christian peace or blood-letting.
> The evil of the Cats, the perfidy of the Galls
> Closed our passage through *Ceolas nam Beuc*.

What a perfect example of an invader's cynical propaganda technique, echoed centuries later in communiqués from, for example, 'a peak in Darien', from Culloden, Abyssinia and Afghanistan.

Incidentally, the 'Cats' were the inhabitants of what are now the counties of Caithness and Sutherland. The 'Galls' were the progenitors of the modern Sinclair family. Ceolas nam Beuc (the 'roaring channel') lies south of the Island of Graemsay in Orkney, at the western end of Scapa Flow.

The story, if not the song, goes on to relate how the Uist men in particular retired from the operation, 'sailing off into the sun'. Their orders from the commander of the expedition were 'not to approach land until Uist would appear to the east of the dawn.' In other words they were to seek the open Atlantic because it would be safer there than in the narrow waters of the Minches.

There is irony in the fact that after so many abortive forays by the MacDonalds, Orkney and Shetland were acquired peacefully by the Scottish crown in 1468, a pledge for the dowry of Margaret of Denmark when she married James III. This would bring little pleasure to the Lords of the Isles, whose dreams had been of personal rather than national conquest.

In the mid sixteenth century, shortly before the Reformation (1560), a conference of church dignitaries and clan chiefs was convened at Dunkeld, with the object of settling the bloody disputes which constantly arose between the king and his nobles. Among those invited was the chief priest of Trinity Temple, a MacVicar, who acted as spokesman for the Church in the Western Isles. He must have made a good impression on members of the conference, because the Bishop of Elgin, who presided, commended him on his grasp of the national situation and offered him the abbacy of Scone in Perthshire. MacVicar, however, politely refused, saying that the people of the Isles were 'more peaceable than those of the Low Countries and much more amenable to reason'. In any case, he believed he could do more good among his own people in North Uist than among Lowlanders in Perthshire.

The impact of the Reformation did not reach the Hebrides for many years. When it did, it met with opposition. In some of the islands it still does.

In North Uist – so the *sennachies* told me – the main opposition came from the MacVicars. Influenced by their ancient ties with Trinity Temple, they regarded themselves as custodians of the old faith and the old customs. The reforming authorities on the mainland decided that as long as the MacVicars retained power there was little chance that the Reformation would succeed in North Uist. They hatched a plot, therefore, to break their power.

At the time, in the late sixteenth century, the greater part of the island was owned and administered by a certain Donald MacVicar (Am Piocair Mor, Big MacVicar) and his four sons. Of those sons Donald had Carinish and Claddach Carinish, Angus the pennylands of Baleloch, Balemartin and Balelone, Hector the lands of Ceolas Bernera and Bale MhicPhail, while John, the youngest, lived with his father, who held the whole island of Baleshare, together with the great hill of Eaval. Each MacVicar occupied a dun on one of the numerous island lochs to which there was access by an artificial causeway.

The remains of such duns, built originally about a

thousand years ago, possibly as places of defence against marauding strangers, can still be seen in North Uist. One of them, in Loch Una near Claddach Kirkibost, is called Dun Ban. I remember well, during that holiday more than sixty years ago, being warned by my father and grandfather not to go near it or, at any rate, not to step on to the causeway. Two boys named MacVicar had lost their lives there; and a whispered prophecy implied that a third MacVicar death in Loch Una was inevitable. (As far as I know this death has not yet occurred. So all young MacVicars, beware!)

In the autumn of 1581 Am Piocair Mor received an invitation from the Privy Council to attend a meeting in Edinburgh, ostensibly so that he might advise them on the political climate in North Uist. His wife tried to persuade him not to go, saying she had a presentiment that something evil was about to happen; but in the end Donald decided it was his duty to go.

Having got Big MacVicar out of the way, the plotters went into action.

At this period in history the MacDonalds of Sleat in Skye had, by force, occupied some lands in North Uist adjacent to those of the MacVicars. Donald Gorm MacDonald, the chief, had appointed as his factor on the island his nephew Hugh MacDonald, 'son of Archibald the Clerk'. Bribed by his uncle with promises of money and territory, and spurred to action by the reforming head of Clan Campbell, Hugh agreed to carry out a cruel plan.

Having collected a strong bodyguard in Skye, he returned to North Uist, landing at Lochmaddy. Then, in the dark and stealthily, he made for Carinish, where he found Big Mac-Vicar's eldest son, Donald, sleeping for the night with his wife and one of their children in a hunting hut. As swiftly and efficiently as any modern hit man, he murdered them all and burned down the hut, which also contained many valuable ecclesiastical and family documents. The remainder of Donald's several children were lucky. It would seem that on the fatal night they were being looked after by servants in the family dun.

Before news of this evil deed could emerge from Carinish

Hugh MacDonald made contact with the other three brothers, offering them his hand in friendship and inviting them to a business meeting at the MacDonald headquarters in Dun an Sticir, another island fort. Guilelessly, Angus, Hector and John accepted his invitation; and that night, as they feasted, the MacDonalds drew their dirks and killed the brothers, one by one.

When Big MacVicar returned home, just before Michael-mas, he found his four sons dead and their holdings taken over by the MacDonalds. Like old MacGregor of the song, he was left 'sonless and landless'. According to the fireside tales he bowed his head and said, 'I am over sixty years of age and never thought to see such evil and wickedness perpetrated in the name of our Saviour. I fear this is only the beginning of much evil and destruction!'

Much evil and destruction did follow in North Uist, as elsewhere, in the name of religion. And Am Piocair Mor would have found no difficulty in understanding the so-called 'troubles' in Northern Ireland today.

The four brothers who died by treachery had three sisters. One of them composed a lament for the brothers, 'Oran Chlann a Phiocair', 'The Song of the Clan MacVicar'. In the original Gaelic it is a cry of agony and vengeance wrung from a woman's heart. It begins:

> Tall man from the Coolin hills,
> Light is your step, strong your blow,
> My seven curses on your foster mother
> That she did not press on you with knee or elbow
> Before you killed all the brothers.

After 1581 the MacVicars became mere tenants and eventually were integrated with the crofting communities in North Uist. They were also persuaded to become Protestants, more to conform with their neighbours' ideas than out of any deep conviction.

When my father used to tell me the story and recite the poem, he would conclude by saying, 'Our family is descended directly from Donald, Big MacVicar. I am Angus, son of Angus, son of Angus, son of Archibald, son of Donald, son of Angus, son of John, son of Donald, son of Angus, son of Donald, son of Donald, Am Piocair Mor.' And having got this proud patronymic impressed on my mind, and having reminded me that my son Jock, christened Angus John, could add two more Anguses at the beginning of *his* list, sometimes he would change the mood and become pontifical.

'A knowledge of our forebears is highly important if we are to understand ourselves and give of our best in the society in which we find ourselves. We can observe their characteristics in our own behaviour and, with luck, learn from their failures, both moral and physical. And, of course, from their successes.

'I think a proof of this argument may be found in our own family: in myself and in yourselves, my five sons and one daughter. I am a preacher. So is your brother Kenneth. Archie and Rona, they were schoolteachers. Willie commanded a ship and John is a Professor of Midwifery. You yourself write books and talk on radio and television, and your son Jock is a newspaperman. We all became teachers and preachers in one way or another, like the thirteenth century MacVicars in Trinity Temple. We all hated to leave home, like the MacVicar priest who was offered and refused the abbacy of Scone. In spite of the fact that nowadays we may all vote differently, as Socialists, Tories, Liberals and Scottish Nationalists, we are all by nature conservative, with an inbred suspicion of change, like Big MacVicar and his sons at the Reformation. And, incidentally, look what happened to them!

'In specific cases the resemblance to our ancestors is striking. Many of the old MacVicars were good shinty players.' (He did not add that many also have been fairly good at shooting a line.) 'I myself played shinty for Scotland, as you know. It came out in Willie's daughter Susan and John's daughter Marsali, who both played hockey for Scotland. Kenneth is minister of Kenmore in Perthshire, not far from Scone. Unlike his ancestor in the mid sixteenth century, he has a high regard for the people there; but he resembles him closely in his attitude to change. When offered the pulpit of a big church in Edinburgh he refused it, on the grounds that the people of Perthshire were more peaceable than those of a big city and more amenable to reason. Or words to that effect!

'What about Willie as the captain of a ship and yourself as a transport officer during the Second World War? Weren't you following in the footsteps of old Donald, who acted as a seafaring quartermaster for the Lords of the Isles?'

By this time in full spate, my father was sometimes interrupted by my mother, herself a MacKenzie from North Argyll. 'Have I no say at all in the characteristics of our family?'

'Of course you have, Mamma. But the MacVicars – well – '

'Are much more important?'

'Now, Mamma, don't you start arguing!'

'I'm not. At any rate, my ancestors fought at Culloden, which is more than yours did.'

'On the wrong side! With the blasted Hanoverians! In any case, the MacVicars were in the Navy at the time!'

But I do believe that a knowledge of one's heredity is important, if only as a measure to guide one's own performance in the exciting game of life. I do believe, also, that it is a good thing to try and break out of its smothering influence as, in fact, my father did.

One thing the MacVicars can say with authority is that they are Celts, in every ancestral direction. And about the Celts the poet Ossian wrote: 'They went forth to the battle, but they always fell.'

My father went forth to the battle; but he himself would never agree that he had even stumbled in the fray.

Out of this background of violence, poverty and sadness the Padre emerged as a vigorous, optimistic and prejudiced man.

He was vigorous in both body and spirit, perhaps because he was a product of a society in which only the fittest survived. He had powerful arms and wrists, the result of youthful digging in the fields and peat hags of North Uist and of much playing of 'the shinty'.

Long before church youth clubs became fashionable, he ran a kind of young man's guild, at meetings of which Sandy

MacCallum gave lessons in carpentry and other crafts which might prove useful to young farmers and young farm labourers. On one occasion the Padre himself produced a three-legged stool. This he presented to Maimie, the maid, who accepted the gift without marked enthusiasm. Her reservations were justified. One night it collapsed underneath her, leaving her sprawling on the kitchen floor in a flurry of skirts and starched apron, and Archie and Willie and I had to flee to the boys' room above not only to utter shrieks of private laughter but also to escape from her snorts of rage and low mutterings, '*Chiall bennachd mi!* Can some folk not stick to their own job of preaching instead of trying to do poor Sandy MacCallum out of a job!'

What I remember equally vividly about the guild were the parties held in the Manse to mark the end of each session. Games of many kinds were played, including one called 'Fire, Air, Water', a rumbustious affair at which enormous young men – enormous, that is, to my childish eyes – leaped and hurled themselves about, causing danger to my mother's furniture. Indeed, during one particularly violent scramble a sofa leg was broken off, much to everybody's dismay. Dryly my mother remarked, 'Well, let's see how good you all are at carpentry! Can't you repair it?' Sadly, my father and the other young men had to admit that Sandy MacCallum's expert hand would be required for the job.

Another ploy at the guild parties was a hand-wrestling competition, at which the contestants faced each other, elbows on a table, forearms upright, hands clasped in powerful opposition. The winner's task was to force his opponent's forearm flat down on the table. Much to the chagrin of all the agricultural strong men – and to my secret pride – the Padre always emerged as the champion, a fact which probably did as much for his Christian influence in the parish as a year's sermonizing.

It became obvious at an early stage that he wanted his children to equal him in physical fitness. Often he made us accompany him on his parish visitations, which, as a rule, entailed long walks in rough country. He insisted also that we should help him in the garden, digging, hoeing, planting potatoes and sawing down trees. Sometimes we felt considerable resentment when he left us to work by ourselves and went off, as he explained, to attend to 'parish business'. Only by slow degrees did we come to understand that sustained physical labour was not suited to his volatile temperament.

He encouraged us, too, to become athletes and was full of enthusiasm when my brother Archie won a soccer blue at his own old university and my sister Rona won a blue for lacrosse at Edinburgh. When we competed at local Highland games he shouted us on, uninhibited by false modesty; and when I won the 100 yards at the age of sixteen he boasted to his elders, 'He's even faster than I was at his age!'

He was optimistic, in face of much evidence to the contrary, that his message of Christian love was bearing fruit in Southend. Towards the end of his forty-seven years as minister of the parish he was in the habit of saying, 'Things are always getting better. Living conditions have improved beyond recognition since I was inducted here in 1910. Poverty is being eradicated. There is a concern for the old and the sick and for the well-being of children, which was conspicuous for its absence at the beginning of the century. The value of education, both theoretical and practical, is now recognized even by the most reactionary of landed proprietors. In days to come there will be even greater blessings.' In Southend, as I discovered, he had done a great deal himself, as a preacher of the Word and as a member of the Argyll County Council, to alleviate the situation of his parishioners.

On rare occasions, however, when some favourite scheme of his had crumbled to disaster, his optimism would be overwhelmed by a mood of black despair. Strangely enough, this did not result in his becoming sadly resigned like his Hebridean ancestors. On the contrary, it caused him to utter loud diatribes against those he considered guilty of wrecking his plans and to contemplate terrible revenge against them. Afterwards he would express shame for his actions, though we soon came to realize that such shame was not always sincere.

He was prejudiced against people he called 'holy willies', some of them his fellow ministers: people he described as having 'one face for the Sabbath and another for weekdays'. A Free Church minister, distantly related to himself, was one I remember who incurred his wrath. Asked to assist at a summer communion in Southend, this stout divine preached hell fire for those who drank to excess and then had three helpings of rich plum pudding at lunch, leaving my mother with none. Afterwards he called her 'a frivolous creature' because on the Sunday afternoon she took Archie and me for a walk and helped us to gather wild flowers by the riverside. 'I hate a man like that,' snarled the Padre, which said little for his Christian charity but a great deal to indicate that his roots were deeply embedded in the old Christian precepts of hospitality and tolerance.

The Rev. Kenneth MacLeod of Gigha, author of the song 'The Road to the Isles', once described the Padre and himself as being one third Protestant, one third Roman Catholic and one third pagan. There was truth in this. Steeped as they were in the traditions of the Celtic Church, which still retained traces of Druidic superstition and wasted little time in discussing fine points of doctrine, they both believed that ecumenical arguments bore small relevance to Christ's universal message: 'Love thy neighbour.' And in this context 'neighbours' indicated not only Protestants and Roman Catholics but also pagans.

It is significant that in many Hebridean islands today Protestants and Roman Catholics live in quiet harmony and, if left to themselves by their respective leaders, would worship together willingly and without embarrassment. It is significant, too, that when I was in North Uist, sixty years ago, my father told me that one old lady, speaking in the Gaelic, had asked him on the first Sunday, 'Are you going to the stones?' She meant, 'Are you going to church?' But she was echoing the question of an ancestor who had lived thousands of years ago and who worshipped with the Druids at a place marked by tall, still-standing megaliths.

He was prejudiced also against those of wealth and high position who did not support his view of Christianity. The

Dowager Duchess of Argyll and Mrs Boyd of Carskiey did not, of course, come into this category. They counted themselves among his parishioners and gave liberally to church funds, and their attitude to less fortunate neighbours was, in his opinion, sufficiently humble and sincere. But there were others, especially descendants of the great landowners who had engineered the Clearances, for whom he had an unswerving disregard.

In the early nineteenth century ancestors of his own had been dispossessed of their crofts in North Uist in order to make way for sheep, and stories recounting similar deeds of shame in Sutherland and Argyll had been told to him around the peat fire in his father's house. In the sixteenth century the Clan Donald had killed the sons of Big MacVicar and taken their lands: in his pocket book he kept a copy of the poem which recorded the tragedy, 'Oran Chlann a Phiocair'. Like a true Celt, if not a true Christian, he had no intention of forgiving and forgetting. The Church of Scotland ministers who had supported the noble lairds in their eviction plans, preaching to their people that they must submit to 'the will of God' and emigrate, were the subjects of his most virulent criticism. 'They sold their souls for a mess of potage!' he would thunder. 'They depended on the generosity of the lairds for their stipends and so put greed for money before all Christian principles.'

And yet he had no time, either, for these ministers who, at the Disruption in 1843, broke away from the Church of Scotland and founded the Free Church in order to release the clergy from such patronage. Like his ancestors who had resisted the Reformation, he had a feeling for continuity and tradition. He used to quote a saying of his grandfather, who had witnessed the clearances in North Uist and been an elder of the Church at the time of the Disruption: 'My Church, right or wrong! And in any case, ministers never made or marred it!'

The Padre was prejudiced against all false prophets. This prejudice I have inherited: and I am glad he did not live to become apoplectic about some of the most modern examples of the species. They are not ministers of the Church. They are to be found amongst politicians and amongst those who call themselves, variously, advertising agents and public relations officers.

Within recent years, the originators of a brilliantly success-ful publicity campaign on behalf of the American television series, 'Dallas', tried to make us all believe that a question of huge importance to every man, woman and child in the civilized world was this: 'Who tried to kill J.R.?' (J.R. was J. R. Ewing, an oil-rich villain whose style and smile we were supposed to admire and love.) Aided and abetted by ladies and gentlemen of the media terrified of missing out on a new cult – and by bookies naturally eager to prise even more money out of the pockets of the gullible – they planted the question in well-tilled fields and reaped the harvest.

Of money, that is: money, the god of modern man, to whom, as the Padre used to say, the idea of profit appears to have become more sacred than love or compassion or friendly argument. Great megaliths have been erected in its honour, labelled TUC and CBI. Governments bow down before them, apparently oblivious to Christian voices plead-ing: 'Love thy neighbour. Have respect for the dignity of others.' (But I don't blame the governments, entirely. *We* elected them. *We* are to blame, especially those amongst us who profess the antediluvian creed that politics and religion don't mix.)

Acolytes of the great god are the hidden persuaders, the pressure groups of various kinds. They compete fiercely against one another, and there is nothing wrong with that, just as there is nothing wrong with alcohol, provided it is used with discipline. What is becoming more and more frightening are the methods sometimes employed to achieve their ends: methods which are now so common that society appears to have become blind to their inherent hypocrisy and dishonesty.

We listen and snigger with grudging admiration and tell one another: 'It's the way of the world.' It may be the way of some people in the world; but are we all too 'wet' to understand it is not the way of Christianity?

Take the now almost forgotten Rhodesian sanction

busters. A few small firms were pounced upon; but some big multinationals got away with it, partly because they were financially too powerful even for governments to tackle and partly because pressure groups supporting them – inside and outside parliament – were able to persuade us that sanctions were against our national interests and that, therefore, a blind eye might wisely be turned upon them. The truth is now clear. Such pressure groups helped to prolong the strife in Zimbabwe for more than a decade and were, therefore, in some degree responsible for the deaths of thousands of people, both black and white.

Take the unfortunate business in 1980 of the British Lions' tour of South Africa, followed by the equally unfortunate business of the Olympic Games. The roars of indignation uttered by Colonel Bogey in the clubhouse bar at the idea of rugby players being denied their sport in a country which killed and tortured in the name of apartheid were suddenly transformed into roars from the same colonel at the idea that athletes should pursue their sport in a country which killed and tortured in the name of Communism. The cry of 'You can't bring politics into sport', uttered, for example, by the Prime Minister's husband, was drowned by a subsequent cry from the Minister for Sport, 'You can't keep politics out of sport.'

It is obvious, if our will to oppose apartheid and Communism stops short of physical warfare, that our only other weapon is sanctions, both spiritual and material. At the same time I detest the thought of idealistic young sportsmen being pressured into making sacrifices when those who continue to trade with South Africa and Russia are asked to make none. (At the time of the 1980 Olympic Games, according to Customs sources, British exporters were using Russian supply routes to ship three million pounds worth of vital goods to the Soviet side in Afghanistan. In addition to large quantities of spares and motor oil, the exports included textiles, miscellaneous metal products, clothing and food. Some 60 per cent of the goods were sent by ship to Leningrad and then taken by rail to Termez and Kushka, on the Soviet–Afghan border. The rest was air-freighted to Kabul.)

Who tried to kill J.R.? In time, all those interested received an answer.

For us today there is a more appropriate question. Who is trying to kill the Christian ethic? Are we seeking in all good faith the answer to that one?

But all this philosophizing, which I know is prejudiced and even unChristian, has run far ahead of the story of a boy growing up in a country manse. Neither radio nor television existed then, and the only newspaper I ever saw – but seldom read, except for the football results – was the *Glasgow Herald*. And yet, perhaps in childhood I had a clearer view of the springs of human behaviour than I have now in crabbed age, bemused as I am by the voices and the writings of numerous experts on the subject, so few of whom seem to agree.

There is one thing certain. The boys of sixty years ago had no worries concerning money or the employment of their leisure time. They seldom possessed even a penny to worry about; and, luckily, recreation was always free in the fields and on the shores of the Mull of Kintyre.

7. Ginger in my Genes

My father's parishioners were mainly farmers and farm labourers. It was fortunate that his own background, as a crofter's son, enabled him to talk knowledgeably about crops and cattle and relate the care of the land to his Christian message.

'He shall feed his flock like a shepherd: he shall gather the lambs within his arms, and carry them in his bosom, and shall gently lead those that are with young.' This was a favourite text of his, one which, in his view, must be in tune with the practical experience of many of his congregation. 'As your minister,' he said once, 'I am a kind of assistant shepherd. My work is to feed you in a spiritual sense and care for your immortal souls.'

His kirk treasurer at the time was Hugh MacEachran, tenant of the arable farm of Kilblaan across the river from the Manse. Brusque, red-bearded, sparing with compliments, Hugh had an Old Testament vision of Christianity which brooked no easy options for backsliders. His care of a few pennies in the collection plate was as strict as that of the Bank of Scotland in dealing with millions of pounds. After my father's pulpit flight of fancy, I overheard one hill farmer chuckle to another, 'Ay, maybe MacVicar's no' a bad assistant shepherd, but man, in ould Hughie he hes a gran' workin' doag!'

And, indeed, like a collie with straying sheep, Hugh was inclined to bully his fellow elders when, in his opinion, they failed in their duty. The spiritual aspect of his discipline must remain in doubt because of his habit of swearing, a habit of which my parents believed he was innocently unaware. There was the Sunday, at turnip-thinning time in June, when a young elder, handing round the wine at a communion service, overlooked the occupants of a long pew near the east door of the church. 'Ye stupid young bugger,' said Hugh afterwards, 'ye missed a bloody drill!' (The Padre heard; but his ear remained Nelsonian.)

In summer, Archie and Neil MacLean and I enjoyed many days out at 'the clippings'. Those were organized on a cooperative basis, with dates set aside for individual farms, when all available sheep hands in the district foregathered to shear the fleeces from hundreds of ewes and 'gimmers' in a single day.

Sometimes my father included such dates in his 'Intimations' from the pulpit. His rule was to avoid making what he called 'secular announcements'; but he had a soft spot for the shepherds and occasionally broke it in their favour. I think his carefulness in this respect stemmed from a story he once heard from a colleague in the Lowlands, a story he subsequently loved to tell at weddings and other public functions.

One day, in his vestry before the morning service, the Lowland minister was approached by one of his elders, an old farmer who was almost stone deaf. 'Minister, wad ye intimate that last nicht I lost a young cattle beast frae the laich meedow?'

'All right, John.'

'An' wad ye ask the folk tae keep a guid look oot for her?'

'Certainly.'

'An' seein' I'm a wee thing deef, wad ye gi'e the pulpit a bit dirl when ye mak' the intimation, so as I'll ken ye've done it?'

'I'll do that, John. Don't worry.'

The time for the 'Intimations' came. The minister began with an announcement that a new district nurse had been appointed. 'I hope,' he said, 'that she will receive from all of us the warmest of welcomes. Our parish has the reputation of being one of the kindest and most hospitable in the Lowlands. Let us remember this when a young and somewhat inexperienced girl enters the community.' And to emphasize the point he struck his hand hard on the pulpit board.

Sitting in the front pew, hearing nothing, old John saw the gesture and took it for the promised 'dirl'. Excitedly he rose to his feet. 'An' ye'll ken her fine if ye see her,' he told an entranced congregation. 'She's got a big broon spot on her belly, an' she's in calf!'

My father, when talking in a casual way, had a genius for messing up the punch line of a story. I have it too, much to the embarrassment of my nearest and dearest. In his case it must have been caused by the fact that he did most of his thinking in the Gaelic. When he told the story of old John and the district nurse – which he did so often that everybody in Southend knew it by heart – his listeners always waited with joyful anticipation for the denouement. Chuckling heartily to himself, he would repeat the words of old John: 'An' ye'll ken her fine if ye see her. She's got a big broon calf in her belly, an' she's – she's got a spot!' Whereupon, his audience would explode into delighted laughter and the Padre would remark to my mother, 'They fairly enjoyed that one, Mamma!'

But back to an old-time clipping in Southend.

For the individual sheep farmer and his men the day always began at first light, when the sheep whose wool was to be shorn were slowly gathered in from the hills. By breakfast time, thanks in the main to strenuous efforts by well-trained collies, the task was complete, and a dozen or more neighbours were in position on triangular wooden stools, exchanging current gossip and honing their shears in readiness for a long day's darg.

The youngest members of the party – shepherds' sons and daughters and stray adventurers like ourselves, along with a few young men of the parish on summer vacation from the university – had a special job to perform. We caught the sheep in the pens, dragged them on to the nearest vacant stool, then turned them over on their backs so that the clipper might secure their feet with special leather straps and make the first thrust with his shears into the thick wool on their bellies.

Procuring the sheep was not easy. We had to select our animal, catch it, get astride it and, with hands gripping its horns, haul it between our legs a distance of anything up to thirty yards. For a boy of eleven or twelve, no matter how physically fit, those bucking, squirming ewes, temporarily separated from their lambs, were hard to handle. Many a time, as we struggled to bring them to the waiting clippers, they would kick up their hind legs, strike our bottoms with their hard rumps and send us sprawling over their heads. Then we had to recover, dust ourselves down and chase and catch them again, while the shepherds roared with laughter and uttered ribald jokes at our expense. Often we felt bruised and battered and almost exhausted; but it was a point of honour to try and show no weakness.

Sometimes, however, on account of the numbers present, we were able to work a rota system, whereby, after the first flush of enthusiasm declined, a few of us could take time off. On those occasions we liked to sit with the collies, which were also resting, and fondle and speak to them until warned by the shepherds to leave them alone and not spoil them.

We also liked to watch the shepherds wielding their shears. (At that time each man owned his own shears, honing them and oiling them with loving care. Now they mainly use electric clippers, hired for the occasion.) The speed at which they worked astonished us. With three or four powerful cuts the underside of the sheep was done. Then they turned it over and dealt with the upper part of its body. If it happened to be nicked by the shears, the clipper bent down and, with a short stick, took a gout of Archangel tar from a tin and smeared it on the wound. In seconds, it appeared, the whole fleece was lying beside the stool and the sheep, released and bleating loudly, was being chivvied towards the pen. There, naked as a skinned rabbit, it was immersed in a long, deep trough filled with sheep dip, after which it was driven out, back on to the hillside – no doubt, considering the undignified treatment it had undergone, to its immense relief.

Meanwhile, one of the older shepherds lifted the fleece and handed it up to the man in charge of 'the bag'. This bag, about ten feet in height, was suspended from a kind of gallows consisting of two tall wooden poles surmounted by a crosspiece. To begin with, the charge hand operated from a ladder propped up against the gallows. As it gradually filled, however, he stepped from the ladder into the bag in order to stamp down the contents.

The noise was constant and exciting: the bleating of sheep, the shouting of men, the laughter when one of us boys took a tumble, the frustrated barking of collies when small boys joined them in rounding up a sheep that had tried to escape from the pens. The smells were constant, too: of sheep dip, of tar, of the sheep themselves, of sweating men. The scene was one of continual movement as bright shears flashed, as men in shirt sleeves and gallowses (braces) directed shorn sheep into the splashing dip trough, as panting boys wrestled with recalcitrant ewes. I can hear and smell and see·it all even after sixty years.

At midday there was a lull while the host shepherd and his womenfolk served an outdoor lunch. This usually consisted of huge cheese and meat sandwiches washed down with equally huge glasses of whisky and water or, for the less mature, of lemonade. During this time, soon after the First World War, at a price of approximately 35p per bottle in modern money whisky was relatively cheap.

But it was when the day ended, about seven o'clock in the evening, that I enjoyed myself most. Everybody tramped into the farm kitchen, a cool, airy place with a polished stone floor and strips of dried cod hanging from the ceiling beams. We sat round scrubbed wooden tables, talking and laughing with relief at work well done. Great bowls of Scotch broth, containing coarse barley, diced turnips and carrots, shredded cabbage and fresh green peas, were set before us, followed by plates of steaming mutton stew with new potatoes. For dessert, if anyone had space left in a violently distended stomach, there might be curds and cream accompanied by stewed gooseberries. The food matched keen appetites, and our appreciation was measured by a continuous slurping and smacking as we consumed it.

Afterwards, when dusk began to gather and paraffin lamps were lit, the older men lit their pipes and over an unlimited supply of whisky began to tell the stories and the jokes which held me spellbound. It reminded me of the *ceilidh* nights in my grandfather's house in North Uist, though the talk here was generally louder, more self-assured, without the Hebridean undertone of sadness.

As a rule, the oldest man present was Archie Campbell, a tenant shepherd with the Duke of Argyll and a parish councillor. His wit was keen, and nobody ever tried to argue with him for fear of a verbal whipping. And yet he loved a joke, even at his own expense, and he was always courteous and kind to women and children. His descent was from the MacNeills, an aristocratic family in the Mull of Kintyre – no doubt connected with the kingly O'Neills of Antrim across the water – and his precise and careful speech was evidence of this.

One day my father, my brother Willie and I went visiting to Dalsmirren where Archie lived with his sister Rosie and brother Ned. As soon as we entered the house, following a traditional rule of hospitality, a bottle of whisky was placed on the table and, beside it, a jug of milk.

'And now, minister,' said Archie, 'after your long walk you will be having a wee dram?'

'Thank you, Archie.'

'And you, Angus?' pointing to me, aged ten.

'A glass of milk, please.'

Then to Willie, aged five, 'And what about yourself, *laochain*? Tell me what you'd like.'

Willie pointed at the whisky bottle.

Archie's round, white-whiskered face broke into a happy smile. 'Ah!' he said, patting my brother's head. 'There's a great future in front of *you*, my boy!'

Having tramped the hills and glens of Southend for so many years as a shepherd, Archie had a store of knowledge concerning the Bronze Age duns and the even more ancient Neolithic chambered cairns hidden away in remote corners of the parish.

After one clipping I remember listening with a strange stirring of excitement to a story he told about the big stones arranged in the shape of a heart in the hills above Dalsmirren. They lie beside a hill road leading to Campbeltown, and Archie brought silence into the kitchen as he described how, on his way home from the town on a moonlit night, he had seen shadows moving around the stones in a silent dance. 'I was not afraid,' he said. 'I stood there, watching, and felt that maybe I should be joining them, even though I knew quite well that what I was seeing must have happened five thousand years ago. Then a cloud came over the moon and the shadows disappeared. It was then that I was afraid, and a great loneliness came on me.'

Coming from anyone else around that table such a story might have caused sceptical laughter; but nobody laughed at Archie. In a dim way I understood even then the feeling he was trying to convey to us: an awareness of our links with prehistory; an awareness that people in the Neolithic Age must have been very like ourselves, their ancient settlements and places of burial clear evidence that the ideal of community existence is by no means a modern concept; an awareness that such community existence, in which people share with one another not only food but also joys and sorrows, is the mark of caring humanity as against that of the animal world which is always callously material.

It was this story, told by a jolly, down-to-earth pragmatist like old Archie, which, I think, caused my initial interest in the prehistory of my parish community: an interest which still gives me pleasure and excitement as I explore the hills at the Mull of Kintyre looking for more evidence of the men, women and children who lived in Southend long before the first pyramid was erected in Egypt. In North Uist stories concerning my family went back seven hundred years. They gave me insight into the question: 'Who am I?' Now, in my imagination, I can conjure up pictures of the wider human family which go back seven thousand years. And which add a new significance to the question.

The first human beings known to have lived in Southend – and indeed in Scotland – did so in the age described by archaeologists as Mesolithic. They were active, small-boned hunters and fishermen whose flint arrowheads and spearheads have been found in abundance near the Mull. Not long ago one of their flint workshops, cluttered with rejected

weapon heads, was discovered on a building site in Campbeltown, ten miles away. Their courage in leaving their native
territory in Ireland and crossing the North Channel in boats
made of wicker, hides and clay – or perhaps even of hollowed
out treetrunks – was impressive, though it is interesting to
discover that they always appear to have moved in tribal
groups, never alone.

According to my wife's cousin, the late Andrew McKerral,
who was an archaeologist as well as a noted historian, 'the
discovery of a Mesolithic flint workshop in Campbeltown has
disclosed the fact that this is the first known locality in
Scotland to receive human colonisation'. Southend, being
only eleven miles distant from Ireland at the narrowest part
of the North Channel, can be likened to a pierhead for
groups of adventurers moving out of Ireland into new
territory.

After the Mesolithic men came the Neolithic men (*circa*
3000–2000 BC). They were farmers and probably less mobile
than the Mesolithic hunters, but most of them reached
Southend by sea from Ireland. It is the opinion of some
archaeologists that 'between the Mesolithic and Neolithic
periods there is not only a chronological but also a distinct
cultural gap'. I believe this to be unlikely, because people
always mix and intermarry and argue amongst themselves,
so that chronological and cultural gaps are unknown in any
properly researched history of human development. It seems
that the Royal Commission on the Ancient and Historical
Monuments of Scotland supports this view. One radiocarbon
date is available for Mesolithic remains in south-west Scotland. It is 4050 BC (give or take 150 years) for a coastal site
in Wigtownshire, much later than used to be thought possible; and it forces the Royal Commission to conclude that
'the Mesolithic communities were still occupying the fore-
shore at the head of Campbeltown Loch at much the same
time as the arrival of the earliest Neolithic people in the
peninsula'.

Evidence of Neolithic occupation of Southend and the
surrounding district is plentiful. A paleobotanical investigation has been carried out on the Aros Moss, an area of peat

bog between Campbeltown and Machrihanish, only a few miles across the hills from Southend. Pollen analyses of peat samples show that around 3000 BC, or even earlier, there was a marked decline in elm pollen and a corresponding increase in the frequency of grass and other non-arboreal pollens, in particular of ribwort plantain and similar light-seeking weeds of cultivation. The investigation suggests that in the fourth millennium BC the aboriginal forests of Scotland were being cleared and cultivated by progressive Neolithic farmers.

I can't help feeling that many a furious argument must have arisen as the Mesolithic men, probably content to be described as 'aristocratic old squires', continued to rampage after reindeer, elk and wild boar through the laboriously tilled Neolithic fields. (Is there a clue here to the reason why, in general, we Scots are a nation of inveterate poachers?)

More evidence of Neolithic occupation is provided by their ruined chambered cairns, examples of which are common in Southend. Their builders, being farmers, erected them in fertile areas, in particular the raised beach deposits and alluvial gravels. Generally comparable cairns exist in Northern Ireland, and it is obvious that those ancient grave places had a common architectural origin, conceived on a monumental scale for communal burial over many generations. No two examples are exactly alike, and several, it appears, have had a complicated history.

In their initial form, dating from the early part of the third millennium BC, they probably consisted of a single burial chamber rectangular in shape and of megalithic construction, enclosed in a round or oval cairn. But as time went by and the Neolithic inhabitants of Southend made contact with other tribes from England, Wales and Ireland, the original cairns were enlarged and improved and more than one burial chamber added. As my Neolithic ancestors absorbed outside influences they began to recognize something of the divinity in man and erected tall portal stones at the entrances to their burial grounds, thus paying a kind of tribute to the dignity of death.

Long ago my father took me to see the Neolithic cairn on

Macharioch Hill, about two miles east of the Manse. Now, on a Sunday afternoon in late spring, Jean and I often go back there to experience again the atmosphere of the place.

Peewits call around us. The whins bloom yellow, filling the air with the tang of burgeoning life. The houses of Southend are sprinkled like crumbs in the valley below – a valley which widens out to face the North Channel and the distant backdrop of the Antrim Hills. We stand in the midst of the cairn, the portal stones behind us, the open and empty burial chamber at our feet, and it becomes clear why ancient men chose this place as one where they might contemplate a new awareness of the human situation. Here there occurs a sense of being above mundane anxieties, a feeling of peace in the quiet heart of nature.

A proper uncovering of the life style of Neolithic man in Scotland has only just begun. Controlled digs of their chambered tombs have been comparatively rare. In spite of this, however, experts offer two theories about their habits which appear to be incompatible.

Some experts – those who can be described as orthodox – tell me that the Neolithic men emerged from caves. In due course they built primitive dwellings, reared animals for domestic use and practised agriculture for the first time, propagating a few useful plants like one-corn and emmer, two wild grasses known to be the ancestors of wheat. Laboriously they shaped flint and obsidian to make the crude axes and knives which clutter up museums – though some of those axes, in my opinion, are actually hoes once used for tilling the soil. The same experts tell me that the Neolithic men designed and constructed not only chambered cairns like the one on Macharioch Hill but also great religious centres like Callanish in Lewis and Temple Wood near Lochgilphead in Argyll (and Stonehenge in Wiltshire).

To me, an interested layman, it seems curious that rude and constantly busy farmers, eking out a livelihood from hitherto uncultivated ground, should have been able to spend incalculable time and effort in erecting such enormous monuments. There may, of course, have been a ruling class, among them predecessors of the so-called Druids, who were able to seduce their ignorant subjects into doing long stints of slave labour. But a mystery remains. How did the Neolithic builders suddenly become so highly trained in the dressing and mortising of stone? And how were so many great boulders, some weighing more than fifty tons, transported from distant quarries? As yet nobody has been able even to guess at the location of the quarry from which the Callanish stones were taken.

I suppose it is conceivable that men of the Neolithic Age were capable of building cairns and henges that would present problems to a contractor equipped with every kind of modern, microchip machinery. Now, however, with the publication of some recent lines of thought, mystery is piled on mystery.

Other less conservative experts, among them scholars like Professor Alexander Thom and Dr Rolf Muller, have written books which prove, to their own satisfaction and to that of many professional and lay readers, that some Neolithic monuments were built by highly skilled mathematicians and astronomers. Professor Thom has said, categorically, that 'Neolithic man had an almost incredible knowledge of geometry and astronomy'. He is also convinced that the Callanish stones and the stones at Temple Wood – and other lesser known monuments, some in Southend – were in fact lunar observatories and that their designers could 'work out results in advance that would need the help of a computer today'.

What is the answer to such apparently irreconcilable conclusions? Should the theories of Professor Thom and Dr Muller be correct, how is it that three thousand years after the Neolithic period all this advanced knowledge of astronomy and of stone building had to be rediscovered in Scotland?

I suppose that the asking of such questions is an important part of my 'Scottish' character. In certain circumstances I act like a Druid holding up poetic arms to a rising moon, in others like a boorish savage intent only upon pandering to inbuilt carnal lusts. Why? Do my Neolithic ancestors provide a clue?

Are my pagan ancestors responsible also for the love of mystery and magic so strong inside me, as it is inside so many Scots?

I believe that we Scots, lacking in the main an urban sophistication, are closer to the influences of magic than our metropolitan cousins in places, say, like London. We want to believe in it. We welcome its intrusion into a workaday life because of romantic implications foreign to Anglo-Saxon processes of thought but well understood by us (particularly well by the Celtic element in Scotland).

For example, a great many of us, in the course of our experience, have seen objects in the sky which we could not and cannot explain; but our reticence prevents us talking about them, except to neighbours in quiet corners. Like old Archie Campbell, we have seen shadows moving near the chambered cairns. Like Mary MacAulay we have seen the Fata Morgana and only with reluctance have we sought a scientific explanation for it.

Does an inborn memory of ancient magic help me to understand why I am a writer of imaginative stories and why so many of my fellow Scots (especially Hebridean Scots) are born storytellers and, at the same time, eager listeners? My Neolithic ancestors built cairns to the glory of an unknown god – possibly the sun – and to commemorate their dead. Are they still speaking, through a foggy dew of time, reminding us that there are many things in heaven and earth alien to our modern pragmatic culture and that a proper medical study of our mental as opposed to our bodily processes has scarcely even begun?

Neolithic men were succeeded by Bronze Age men, who, in turn, were succeeded by Iron Age men. That is what the archaeologists say, though I believe the statement is merely a shorthand used for chronological convenience. People don't change at the drop of a date. Their habits, philosophy and outlook on life keep developing slowly over the centuries. Future archaeologists may call us the Oil Age men, but we know that our passions and emotions are similar to those of St Ninian and St Columba, who were born on the fringes of the Iron Age but lived on into a period docketed as Early Christian.

During the millennia which followed the Neolithic Age (that is, from about 2000 BC until the dawn of the early Christian period) the story of my ancestors in Southend is one of gradual progress towards a mode of life in the Bronze Age and the Iron Age which was not much different from that which existed in most of rural Scotland less than two hundred years ago (and in the Hebrides, as I discovered for myself, less than a hundred years ago). The evidence for this comes from Bronze Age burial cairns and Iron Age duns (or forts) which are plentiful in the parish.

In time the practice of collective burials in chambered tombs was replaced by that of individual burials in cists or graves, many of which were covered by round cairns or barrows. The men and the women whose remains have been found were, without exception, of small stature (some of them less than five feet in height), and if the giants of Scottish legend ever did stride across the mountains, archaeologists have discovered nothing of their earthly existence.

Neolithic farmers with stone tools became Bronze Age farmers with bronze tools. It is said by some archaeologists that the method of making bronze was introduced to the 'savages' of Britain by Celtic immigrants from Europe. They, in centuries before, had learned the art from Sumerian and Indian smiths, whose experiments with copper and tin alloys had established the formula. On the other hand, Professor Colin Renfrew, the whizz-kid of modern Scottish archaeology, believes that the knowledge of how to produce bronze was discovered independently in European locations: for example, Czechoslovakia and Spain.

It is certain, however, that the Bronze Age farmers were also fishermen. On flat stones they found ancient cup marks – relics of unknown and even then long forgotten rites – which they used as convenient mortars for the grinding of their shellfish bait. As life became a little more prosperous, the Bronze Age ladies began to spend time on the adornment not only of their persons but also of their household and funerary utensils. Probably unwilling to be outdone in the gentler aspect of life, the menfolk began to shave.

Objects to prove all this have been unearthed in a single cairn at Balnabraid, situated near the east coast of Kintyre, on Southend's boundary with Campbeltown. They include agricultural hoes and knives made of flint, bronze fish-hooks, jet disc beads, food vessels, beakers and cinerary urns (some patterned by ropes tied tightly about them while the clay was still soft), slim and elegant pins made of bone and – the final sophistication – a razor with a bone handle and a bronze blade. I take a short breath of wonder when I realize that the Balnabraid cairn and the objects within it were already in existence long before King Tutankhamen ruled in Egypt.

In the centuries which preceded the coming of Christianity to Scotland it is fairly certain that my ancestors were sun worshippers, under the influence of the learned Druids. (In Southend's old churchyard at Keil almost every gravestone has been erected facing east and the rising sun. Only within recent years has the custom gone into abeyance.) Their fortified settlements were built on high ground above the extensive marshes which at the time bordered the rivers Con and Breckrie. I picture them as hard-working people, herding their cattle and cultivating the stony fields during the day, while at the approach of night, when 'hobgoblin and foul fiend' invaded pagan minds, and wolves, wild boar and other dangerous animals roamed the countryside, they retreated for safety behind the stone walls and thick earthworks of their duns; but the discovery of duns several acres in extent leads me to the conclusion that even at this stage the idea of tribal (or village) communities was already well rooted.

The remains of one such settlement can be seen on a hill called Cnoc Araich, above the Manse of Southend. Dating from about 600 BC to AD 400, it covers more than six acres and is the largest to have been found in Scotland. With the Royal Commission on the Ancient and Historical Monuments of Scotland I share a theory about this dun. On account of its size, may not Cnoc Araich have been the headquarters or principal village of the Epidii (horse people)? And may not the well-known family of MacEachran, still numerous in Kintyre, be the direct descendants of this ancient tribe? (The surname MacEachran has its origins in the Gaelic and means 'son of the horseman'.)

By now my ancestors in Southend had become a mixed race, deriving their blood from the small and active hunters of the Mesolithic era, from the dour, hard-working Neolithic farmers and from the warrior Celts, tall and fair, who were described by ethnologists as Goidels (or Gaels) and whose language was the original of Scots and Irish Gaelic and Manx.

During the past two thousand years the Gaels have become the dominant race of Celtic Ireland and the western lands of what is now Scotland; but the genes of the Mesolithic and Neolithic men persist. This is evident in many local families, including Jean's and my own. Jean herself and her surviving brothers are squarely built and dark. But another brother, John, was tall, with light brown hair. In the MacVicar family my brother Archie was tall and fair, like Kenneth, but Willie and John, as Rona was, are stocky and only of medium height, though their colouring remains blond.

It is clear that ancestors are of primary importance in any assessment of my 'Scottishness'; and because of this another question comes bubbling to the surface. Where did my Mesolithic, Neolithic and Celtic ancestors come from?

Few experts are pedantic about the origin of the Mesolithic men; but on the subject of their Neolithic successors prehistorians and archaeologists provide me with contradictory answers.

Professor Gordon Childe believes that they came from Spain, southern France and Sardinia, a short and powerful people, probably dark-skinned and with an oriental cast about their eyes. They were not Aryans, and prehistorians call them by a variety of names: Turanian, Silurian, Iberian. It has been suggested that they still survive as a community in the Basques, whose strange and complex speech, unlike any other in Europe, may be a development of their ancient language.

Another scholar, Dr L. A. Waddell, has written a book called *Phoenician Origin of Britons, Scots and Anglo-Saxons* which 'proves' that my Neolithic ancestors were Phoenicians. The pillar of his argument is the Newton stone in Aberdeenshire. Standing in the grounds of Newton House, under the grey crags of Bennachie (at the back of which, according to the song, there 'rins' the river Gadie), it has two inscriptions, one in Gaelic Ogam, the other in what Dr Waddell believes is Phoenician script. He has translated both and finds that they echo each other: 'This sun-cross was raised to Bil [or Baal, the god of sun-fire] by the Kassi of Silyur of the Khilani, the Phoenician Ikar of Cilicia.' To confuse the issue further, Dr Waddell declares that the Phoenicians were descended from Aryan Hittites.

Modern archaeologists scream with horrified amusement when Dr Waddell is mentioned. But his argument appeals to my imagination.

There is not so much argument, however, about the origin of the Celts – the Gaels who gave their name to my native county of Argyll (Earradh Gael, 'the coastline of the Gael'). A widely held theory is that they came from Asian country north-west of the Indus, Aryan tribes seeking lebensraum in the west and driving before them people of the Neolithic culture. Four thousand years ago they filled and possessed the rich, arable lands of Central Europe.

Then it seems that the Huns arrived, also from Asia, and that they, in turn, drove the pioneering Celts farther to the west. Dr Agnes Mure MacKenzie writes: 'By the time the Greek tragedies were written, when Rome was becoming mistress of Italy – the fourth century before Christ – bronze-using Celts had reached as far as the Orkneys: they may have worked north from the southern part of the island, or come overseas from the Weser and the Rhine.'

Following them there came to our island another race of Celts, the users of iron. They were the Gauls, who gave the Romans such a heap of trouble. Their descendants, the Brythons, settled in Wales and Cornwall, Cumberland and the south-west of Scotland between Clyde and Solway. Their name lingers on in 'Britain' and 'Briton'; and their hatred and suspicion of continental Rome, transmitted down the echoing centuries, may be one reason for a less than enthusiastic response in those areas to the Common Market referendum.

I am, therefore, an Asian, perhaps also an African, and certainly a European with Celtic and Gaulish connections. I am also a Norseman, because of the Vikings who raided and settled in the Hebrides and Argyll in the dark ages between the ninth and thirteenth centuries. This is the extraordinary foundation of my 'Scottishness', a fundamental reason, perhaps, for the chaotic mixture in my character of weakness, aggression, superstition, practicality, suspicion, trust, timidity and adventurousness.

But I like to believe that in the main my characteristics are derived from a Celtic tribe called the Scotti. In the Iron Age, speaking the Celtic language, they began to cross the North Channel from Ireland and infiltrate the territory of the Epidii in Southend. They brought with them St Columba and a brave new religion called Christianity. They gave their name to Scotland – and to me, a Scot.

A Scot? In a narrow sense, yes. In a wider and more humble sense, simply another member of the human race.

8. Farmers' Glaury

('Glaury', not 'glory'. The distinction will become clear.)

I know that the digression from the subject of farming at the Mull of Kintyre, in search for answers to the questions 'Who am I?' and 'Who are we all?', has been a long one. It may, however, have been necessary. Archaeology is a subject which helps to eliminate the narrow fences erected by nationalists and sectarians of every colour. I admit that I am an occasional fence-builder myself; but at any rate I hope I can recognize my errors and struggle to overcome them.

Sixty years ago, when I played hide-and-seek with other boys and girls in their parents' stackyards, most farmers were untroubled by such philosophical problems. They had too many other problems of a mundane character to worry about. They were poor, both in a material and spiritual sense; and their main concern was the wresting of a living for themselves and their families from soil inclined to be inpoverished owing to constant unscientific cultivation over centuries.

Their state was less primitive than that of the North Uist folk. Their holdings were bigger, and they lived in a less isolated situation, with Glasgow only a few hours away by coach, steamer and train. But in order to pay the high rents demanded by the Duke of Argyll and other landowners – especially for mixed arable farms – they had to work throughout almost every daylight hour, with few mechanical aids and with agricultural prices kept deliberately low by governments obsessed with the idea of industrial advancement. (In 1910, the year my father came as minister to Southend, the rent of Lephenstrath, at less than 300 acres one of the largest farms in the parish, was over £400, roughly similar to what the tenant was paying forty-five years later, when the duke sold most of his farms and, at a stroke, allowed the farmers to become landowners in their own right.)

Their education was better than that of their Hebridean neighbours; but at the same time the majority had left school at the age of twelve and their knowledge not only of the world in general but also of scientific methods of farming was rudimentary. With a few exceptions they could be classed as peasants.

The contrast between such farming conditions in Southend and those appertaining today is startling. A revolution has taken place, a revolution only partly camouflaged by the farmers' habit of continual grumbling. (They are not alone in this. When, in the past few years, has anyone heard a member of the CBI or the TUC boast of his prosperity?)

The revolution may be said to have begun soon after the First World War with the introduction of the Kentish white clover, which tended to improve the fertility of clay-based soils. Then around 1930, when milk was being sold by farmers for the pitiful price of threepence ha'penny per gallon (old money), the government stepped in with a Milk Marketing Board and began to distribute farming subsidies, loans and grants. Agricultural colleges and agricultural advisers brought new methods to bear, with beneficial results.

Of course the farmers of Southend, like farmers everywhere, protested loudly at the number of forms they had to fill in; but, in fact, since that time they have never looked back in a material sense. And when, in 1955, the impoverished Duke of Argyll was forced to sell most of his farms to the sitting tenants, the revolution was almost complete. (One farm bought by the tenant in 1955 for £2500 recently changed hands for £250,000.) Money now became plentiful for the purchase of modern mechanical implements of every kind. Great troops of farm labourers were made redundant.

The ploughing used to be done by horses and single-furrow ploughs. Weeks and even months were needed to cultivate the fields. Now heavy tractors yoked to double- and sometimes triple-furrow ploughs can do the job in days, if not hours. The day has already come when a well-heeled farmer, reclining indoors on a comfortable window seat, can press a series of buttons and direct an unmanned ploughing unit in a field half a mile away.

I remember men with wooden seed trays strapped to their chests trudging hour after hour along the furrows, sowing the oats and the barley. A sweep of the right hand, a sweep of the left: the rhythm had to be maintained unbroken, to ensure an even scatter of seed. There were the good sowers and the bad sowers; and even as a boy I formed the theory that a good sower had to be musical, with a keenly developed sense of timing. My wife's brothers, Archie and Davie, were prize-winning singers at many a music festival. They were also experts at sowing by hand. (I believe that good golfers also benefit by having an ear for music. I have played with many top-class amateurs and a few professionals; but the most elegant, most perfectly timed shots ever played against me were by Laurence Glover, the concert pianist.)

But now the hand sowers have been replaced by tractor-drawn machines which insert the seeds in inch-perfect symmetry. As for turnips, which used to be grown for cattle feed, they are seldom sown at all. Hay crops, too, have become scarce. Silage has taken over, and soaring silage towers give farm steadings the appearance of factories, which in a way they have become.

It may be interesting to record that it was a Southend man, Peter MacKay, who worked for a time as an engineer with a Campbeltown shipbuilding company, who invented the 'ruck lifter'. This was a tall contraption formed of three legs of wood mounted on castor-type wheels, which could be man-oeuvred into position around and above the hay ricks. At the apex of the pyramid thus formed was a block and tackle, through which ran a wire rope with three dangling iron hooks. The hooks were inserted under the base of a rick and the wire, when pulled by a horse, lifted the whole rick into a cart, thus saving many man-hours of forking and building. Peter MacKay failed to patent his invention, with the result that though his rick lifter became a common item of agricultural equipment throughout the country, he made no profit from it whatsoever.

The harvesting of oats and barley – oats for animal feed, barley for the many distilleries then flourishing in Campbeltown – used to be a long and laborious process. Sometimes, on account of wet and stormy weather, it lasted from the end of August even into November. (Old Hugh MacEachran, the kirk treasurer, used to say, 'If ye miss the tid an' let the equinoctial gales at the en' o' September catch up wi' ye, then ye'll ha'e a late hairvest.')

The crops were cut by horse-drawn reapers and bound into sheaves by small platoons of hired harvesters, some of them tinkers, like old Danny, earning a quick penny and living in tents on the farms. If a farmer and his men happened to strike lucky and complete their harvest early, they went *en masse* to help less fortunate neighbours. Archie, Willie and I were often enlisted at weekends to help the laggards. Some farmers we enjoyed working for: at the end of a day's work, which usually consisted of tossing sheaves into a procession of carts for conveyance to the stackyard, they might slip us each a precious half-crown. Others simply took our assistance for granted; and if we complained to our mother about their parsimony she would reply, with some severity, that surely the satisfaction of doing good unto others was sufficient reward. In those days, when the idea of weekly pocket money for children had still to be conceived by budding trade unionists, such a high-minded philosophy offered us but small comfort.

I was six years old when the first binder appeared in the parish. This machine, though still drawn by horses (usually three heavy Clydesdale mares), cut and gathered the corn, bound it with special twine and spewed out the resultant sheaves into stooks which were then stacked. It caused me surprise that in spite of his old-fashioned, Old Testament vision of life, it was Hugh MacEachran who purchased Southend's first binder.

Now, of course, binders are obsolete. Combine harvesters, giant, diesel-powered mobile factories, crawl through the

fields of barley and oats, cutting, gathering, threshing and
filling bags with grain in one comprehensive operation. At
present a harvest is sometimes completed in three days,
whereas, in my boyhood, it often took three months. And no
longer does a farmer need to clutter his barn with a crude
threshing machine, often powered by a water wheel mounted
against the outside wall and invariably equipped with
dangerous flying belts and unprotected gear-wheels. Even
cruder and more dangerous hand-operated machines for
slicing turnips and riddling potatoes have also disappeared.

On the dairy side, farming in Southend has also undergone a dramatic change. Before the modern era of silage and
lush, scientifically nurtured grass, a medium-sized farm of
about 150 acres could support an average of only twenty or
thirty cows. Now it is not unusual for a similar farm to have
100 milk cows, plus a full quota of younger cattle.

Before and for some time after the First World War milk
was made into butter and cheese, only a small surplus being
sold to the locally run creamery. Today every drop is carried
away in tankers to a creamery which forms part of a
multinational concern. The result is farming prosperity. It
has also led to an absurd situation in which Jean and I, our
bungalow surrounded by fields of munching, milk-heavy
cows, have to buy tasteless pasteurized milk from the local
shop: milk slopping about in slippery plastic bags which have
come all the way from Glasgow. Is this 'civilization'? Or the
bureaucratic ideal gone haywire? (With waves showering
spray on our windows, and many varieties of marine life
enjoying a carefree existence in the seas around the Mull of
Kintyre, we get most of our fish supplies from Aberdeen,
nearly 300 miles away!)

The people who benefit most from the dairy revolution are
the farmers' wives and daughters. I remember women who
slaved seven days a week at the manufacture of butter and
cheese and, during their period of fertility, bore children at
regular two-yearly intervals. Often they were old and bent
before their time. Work, work, work. Milking the cows by
hand in two-hour operations, one at five o'clock in the
morning, another at five o'clock in the afternoon, each and

every day, each and every week, each and every year. Moving the plunger of the butter churn up and down, up and down for hours on end, with only short intervals of rest for aching arms. Pressing the hardened curd into chisets and heaving those heavy wooden cheese containers from the dairy to the drying and maturing atmosphere of the lofts above. In the evenings knitting, sewing, darning and fashioning clothes for themselves and their children by the light of oil lamps and smouldering peat fires.

There was little or no relief from a drab existence, apart from visits to the church or to Woman's Guild meetings or to Campbeltown on special occasions. The rent had to be paid, and the menfolk had to have their days to market and evenings at the inn. Yet some of those women could smile. They could sing as they worked and could take time off to spread us a 'piece and jam' when we played with their children.

As for the wives of the agricultural workers, who lived in tiny cottages on the farms, their existence was equally hard. They helped out at 'the milkings' for 2s. 6d. per week and bonuses of butter and buttermilk, potatoes and cheese. The younger ones also worked in the fields. At turnip-thinning time I used to see them crawling along the drills, their druggit skirts ragged and stained with glaur (damp earth), while their babies slept – or sometimes howled – behind a hedge at the end of the field. And yet they, too, could be cheerful. Many a time I have stood in a steaming byre at milking time listening to them singing the old 'come-all-ye" ballads, with the local Irish flavour. (Some of those ballads I remember still and can repeat for the benefit of any youngster in the parish who shows the slightest interest. Unfortunately, such youngsters are few, and I have to depend for an audience on erudite folklorists who occasionally come to explore the outback.)

On the day of a fair or an agricultural show, it was recognized that after they had done the morning milking and churning, the ladies were free to visit Campbeltown where such exciting events were held. The farmers' wives travelled the ten miles in open, high-wheeled horse-drawn 'machines', their Sunday hats held on with woollen scarves. The agricultural workers' wives were sometimes given a lift. More often they walked.

The Southend ladies of today offer an amazing contrast. There is no need for hand-milking. Through an array of rubber tubes, pulsing machines convey milk from the cows' udders straight to enormous, clinically clean containers from which it is eventually pumped into the creamery tankers. It is never actually exposed to the air – or to human eyes, except through small glass windows in the piping system – until it emerges from the pasteurizing plant and is poured into the slobbery plastic bags which cause me so much embarrassment when I do the shopping.

A triumph for hygiene. But though we can be sure in this scientific age that milk is utterly free of tuberculosis and brucellosis, its taste has become neutral, and we cannot produce from it the lovely clotted cream which my mother used to say 'put smeddum' into us. (To a Scot 'smeddum' means virility.)

Nor do the farmers' womenfolk need to worry about their butter or cheese-making. These chores are done in the creameries, sometimes by computer. On account of subsidized farm prices, they have plenty of money to spend. All the clothes required for themselves and their children can be bought at Marks & Spencer's or at a fashionable House of Fraser store. And there is no need for eye-straining needlework by lamplight. The occasional darning of a sock is done in a blaze of electric light.

Many among them smoke, drive fast cars, enjoy a gin and tonic, use the pill and wear smart trousers, all of which would have horrified their grandmothers, whose probable reaction would have been to prophecy their imminent descent to hell. They have time in which to tend their gardens and play golf. Instead of churning and cheese-making they do flower arrangements. Instead of thinning turnips, wearing fustian clothes stained with earth, they appear on the golf course in colourful outfits straight from the advertisement pages of the *Scottish Field*.

The British Women's Amateur Golf Champion for 1981

was Mrs Belle Robertson, a farmer's daughter from Southend. She is trim, athletic, feminine, with a world-wide reputation as a gallant sportswoman. Had she been born sixty years earlier, all her gallantry might have been dissipated in a blur of milking, churning and cheese-making, and this male member of her home club in Southend might never have been able to remark, proudly, 'I have played golf with Belle at Dunaverty ever since she was a little girl.'

Many of the farmers in Southend used to keep their money in a sideboard drawer in the 'good room'. Today they employ the banks to execute financial deals more readily associated with city tycoons. But few of them are interested in accountancy, which has become as important a factor in farming as in every other trade and profession. (Including authorship, I may add, in a sour aside.) But like their fathers and grandfathers, who left difficult, finicky jobs like milking, churning and cheese-making to their wives and daughters, many of them now leave them to cope instead with the hard grind of paperwork.

In the drab days, however, there were farmers who did their best to lighten the work of their ladies.

I was often sent by my mother to collect butter and eggs from Dalmore, about a mile away along the riverside from the Manse. The tenant of this farm was nick-named Owld Yadi. Lean and loud-voiced, even at the age of sixty he presented a patriarchal appearance. His grey beard was long and straggly. His eyes, deep sunk in hollow cheeks, seemed to flash fire. He looked like the prophet Abraham pictured in the big family Bible at the Manse (in which all our birth dates were recorded); but in spite of such a holy association I was scared of him. When I encountered him in the fields or in the farmyard I walked warily, giving him a wide berth as I sought the safety of the kitchen and a warm welcome from his wife and daughter. (I was accustomed to carrying out similar manoeuvres if confronted by his Ayrshire bull.)

One day, approaching Dalmore, I was crossing the apparently deserted farmyard when a roar occurred behind me and Owld Yadi emerged from the barn, waving a knobbly walking stick in my direction: a stick which seemed to threaten dreadful pain and sorrow. Indeed, he looked so dangerous that I took to my heels and made for the fence separating the yard from the open fields beyond.

'Stop! Stop!' he bellowed.

I flung myself at the fence and had almost thrust my way through when the seat of my trousers was caught in the barbed wire. It was like a nightmare. The pounding feet came closer. I could imagine the stick raised high to add to the pain in my bottom.

'Whit are ye daein', ye stupid wee bugger?' The voice crackled like thunder.

I waited for the blows. None came. Instead, I felt his hands on my trousers, extricating me from the wire.

Roughly he clutched my arm and hauled me upright. 'Whit's wrang wi' ye? I was only gaun tae ask if ye wanted a sweetie.'

The relief was so great that I could say nothing. He took a peppermint from his pocket. It was covered with fluff and traces of glaur.

'There ye are noo. Away inside an' the wife'll gi'e ye a piece.'

Still shaking, I took the sweetie and did what I was told. It was revealed to me then what a trapped bird must feel when liberated from a garden net by a loud, enormous human being.

Owld Yadi had surprised me by betraying a glint of kindness behind a grey exterior. He surprised other farmers – and his own family – by his invention and building of a machine for stirring the cheese vat.

In the yard, just outside the dairy, he erected a stout wooden pole, some forty feet high. Through a pulley at the top he threaded a thin wire rope, with a heavy metal weight attached. At the bottom end the rope was wound round a metal shaft. This was connected, through a hole in the wall, with an intricate system of gear wheels inside the dairy. Those wheels operated a flail-like arm which, at speed, accomplished the heavy task of stirring the curd in the cheese vat.

The apparatus worked on the principle of a grandfather

clock. As the weight at the pole top was released, its slow descent caused the shaft to revolve, and the gear wheels inside initiated the movement of the stirring arm. When the weight reached the bottom of the pole, Owld Yadi simply wound it up again and continued the process until the curd had reached a proper consistency.

Once, not long after my discovery that his bellow was worse than his bullying, I asked him to show me the invention in action. He grunted with apparent annoyance at this brash request but immediately set the weight in motion. I watched and listened, fascinated, while he explained the workings in proud detail. I thought it marvellous in its simplicity and effectiveness. I still do. And have often wondered why it was not copied by other farmers.

Owld Yadi was known as one of the many Lowlanders in a Kintyre population which otherwise consisted of families of Highland and Irish descent. His people had come from Ayrshire in the early nineteenth century and since then had farmed successfully in Southend. Apparently he was a Scot of the Scots, with all the dour and abrasive qualities glibly attributed to the Lowland Scots. But, as is often the case, such tab marking camouflaged the truth of his heritage. A hundred years before his family's arrival in Southend, his forebears had come to Ayrshire from Poland, as miners in the coalfields.

We are all 'Jock Tamson's bairns'. The question arises: 'Who was – or is – Jock Tamson?'

In his youth, Owld Yadi had been a champion ploughman, handling his horse and 'high cut' plough with snarling expertise. His son Archie became a champion, too, as did his grandson Andrew. When young Andrew won his gold medal, encouraged by fiendish shouts and threats from his grandfather at the end of the rig, the old man, with pretended reluctance, agreed to have his photograph taken with Archie and Andrew. It appeared in the *Campbeltown Courier* above the caption: 'Three generations of champions.' Owld Yadi did his best not to appear too proud.

His relationship with the Padre was, on the surface, a stormy one. He was a keen but quarrelsome golfer, stumping the fairways of Dunaverty at formidable speed, using half a dozen hickory-shafted clubs tied together with binder twine and cursing the whins and his opponents with equal vigour. On his way to and from the course he often called at the Manse to discuss politics with my father. Cringing behind the door, Archie and I sometimes feared for our parent's safety as his visitor, to emphasize a point, beat his stick on the study table and uttered oaths at the pitch of his voice. It was only later we understood that far from being annoyed Owld Yadi was thoroughly enjoying the argument. As was the Padre.

On his death bed he sent for my father. The knobbly stick was laid aside. The vigorous body lay inert underneath the bedclothes. The loud voice had become a whisper.

For a while he discussed sin with the Padre, trying weakly to argue about it as if it were a political issue. (Which, of course, in a way it is.) Suddenly he caught my father's hand and said, 'Will ye – will ye christen me?'

'Christen you? Weren't you baptized, as a child?'

'No. They forgot.'

There was a cup of water on the table by the bed. The Padre used it to climax a short baptismal service in which he and the old farmer were the only participants. The General Assembly of the Church of Scotland might not have approved; but my father, descendant of the semi-pagan Columban vicars in North Uist's Trinity Temple, wasted no time in worrying about that. He had brought comfort to a dying man. Water sprinkled on the white head had submerged loud argument in meekness and peace.

I listened to the Padre tell his story to my mother soon after it happened. It conveyed to me, if only dimly at my age, that human nature is never simple and that good and evil are often relative terms.

The crude earthiness of agricultural life in Southend sixty years ago was matched by the crude earthiness of its morality.

Poverty and bad housing were prevalent: so there was malnutrition and disease. Drink was a way of escape from harsh reality: so there was drunkeness. Sex provided moments of love in an unloving environment: so, at a time when contraceptives were only known to and used by urban sophisticates, there was illegitimacy. Strangely enough, however, there was little violence, except perhaps for some horseplay among the boys and the young men. And in a small community where everyone, 'gentle and simple', knew everyone else, down to the last quirk in his or her character, habitual thieves did not exist.

In respect of robbery and violence, similar conditions prevail in Southend today. That is one reason why we struggle to retain the parish as a community, against the planners and the bureaucrats in church and state who try to submerge us in the anonymous, characterless mass of a larger unit.

In a rural backwater where organized evening entertainment was then practically non-existent – and dark barns and the moonlit 'rigs o' barley' were invitingly private – illegitimacy among farm servants was accepted as being inevitable and no great fuss was made about it, except perhaps by the 'unco guid'.

It was different for the farmers and the farmers' sons and daughters. When a middle-aged farmer with a wife and family fathered a child on one of his servants, the matter was covered up by a quick money payment and the promise of support for the girl's mother if she agreed to bring up the child. Whispers of scandal ran through the parish; but glasshouse dwellers were unwilling to throw too many large stones.

When a youthful member of the farming community went astray, however, the consequences were often disturbing. As a rule, if the two young people were of equally respectable families, the situation was resolved by a hastily arranged wedding. But there were occasions, if a farmer's daughter became pregnant by a farm labourer, or a farmer's son was named as being responsible for a servant girl's expected child, scandal reached a crescendo and a small hell was let loose. In most of those cases love and not lust was concerned, but this was ignored. Marrying beneath you was not on, and many a marriage that might have proved happy was aborted, as some of the bastards were, in blood and tears.

Inevitably, my parents were involved in such situations. I remember hearing them talk together about the young people in distress, always with sad voices; and I vaguely understood they were on the side of the errants against the hypocrites who could hide behind money and respectable backgrounds.

One evening I found my mother crying. She passed it off, telling me she had a headache. I know now what she was crying about. My father had just returned from visiting a prosperous farm in the parish where a son of the house, about to become the father of a child by his mother's kitchenmaid, had drowned himself in the mill dam behind the farm.

Tragedies of this kind seldom occur today. The climate of morality in Southend has changed, as it has done everywhere else in Scotland, especially in the area of sex. Whether it has changed for better or worse is not the point. The fact remains that it has changed, as a result, in part, of the pill and, in part, of the media's efforts to present society in terms of realism. It can be argued that society now looks upon itself more honestly. But is there any evidence that such honesty is accompanied by more Christian love and compassion than it was sixty years ago?

William Hickey sniggers knowingly about love nests and love children, giving the impression that they represent normality in a 'civilized' society. Does such 'honesty', however, reduce the anguish of the innocent spouse in a divorce case? Does it improve the future lot of equally innocent children, legitimate and illegitimate, who are condemned to face life without the anchor of a stable family? They are 'liberated', of course. But from what?

Beyond the pallisades there lies the jungle; and the jungle is a lonely place, where cries for help can be smothered and remain unheard in the thickness of the undergrowth. There is no permanent escape from humanity: not even in Southend.

Harvest time was the farming season I enjoyed most. The stooks of corn and barley were thrown down so that the sheaves might become perfectly dry in the wind and the sun. Then they were loaded into high-sided horse-drawn carts for conveyance to the stackyards. There they were built laboriously, row upon row, into round, peak-topped stacks which would eventually be thatched with dried rushes.

Everybody worked happily and with a will, because this was the climax to a year of ploughing and sowing and reaping and mowing and,. as long as the weather remained cool and bright, ultimate success was just around the corner.

As Neil MacLean and I grew into adolescence we could play useful parts. We were in demand for the 'forking', a job requiring more muscle power than skill, which consisted mainly of throwing the sheaves up into the carts (using a long, two-pronged fork) as they moved from stook to stook. More difficult and responsible jobs, such as leading the horses with their swaying cartloads through steep and narrow gateways, such as forking sheaves from the carts on to the growing stacks, such as the building of the stacks themselves, all these were left to our elders and betters, the expert farmers.

The danger of delegating one of these tasks to somebody less than competent was demonstrated by the experience of a small, stout farm labourer of advanced years, who, on account of a pointed nose and protruding teeth, was nicknamed the Rat by his fellow workers.

We were taking in the harvest at a farm tenanted by Jean's brother, Archie. (The farm is called Dalbhraddan, from the Gaelic, meaning 'glen of the salmon', though the stream in which the salmon once disported themselves has long since been disciplined into a tiled drain.) Owing to a shortage of labour on this particular day, the Rat had volunteered to be the stack builder.

In the present enlightened agricultural era no stacks are built. Any corn or barley that is grown is dealt with by combine harvesters, the resultant straw being baled and stored in open-sided corrugated-iron sheds. But 'in the vaward of our youth' stacks were built on a foundation of dried bracken, row upon row around a central open shaft which provided ventilation. As a rule, a bag of straw in the shaft was pulled up after him by the builder, to ensure that the size and shape of the ventilation shaft remained constant.

The Rat, however, forgot to provide himself with a straw bag, and it was only when his stack had reached a height of about fifteen feet that he decided to inspect the condition of his shaft. As he crawled inwards to look over the edge, some of the sheaves slipped. With a yell of dismay, he plunged down, out of sight, into the bowels of the stack.

'Hey, get me oot! Get me oot!' The voice was like an echo from a Frankenstein grave.

The rest of us doubled up with laughter. This was the kind of diversion which gave lightness to labour. For weeks it would provide material for jokes cracked at kirk and market: crude jokes concerning rats and rat holes. Indeed, 'the day the Rat fell doon the stack at Dalbhraddan' is still remembered by old men supping beer in quiet corners of Southend's Argyll Arms.

Soon, however, our laughter was subdued by an onset of anxiety. What if the stack were suddenly to collapse inwards upon itself and smother the Rat?

A ladder was placed against it, and Neil, who was nimble and light, climbed up to assess the situation. Gingerly, across the slippery sheaves, he approached the opening through which the Rat had disappeared. A sudden movement in the jerry-built stack caused him to scramble back, quickly, just in time to prevent himself joining the Rat in his dark and dangerous misery.

To the feebly moaning victim he shouted, 'Dinna fash yersel'. We'll ha'e ye oot in a jiffy!'

It was a promise more easily made than carried out. As a last resort we might have taken the stack to pieces, flinging off the sheaves row by row; but throughout such a lengthy operation we reckoned that the Rat would always be in imminent danger of being crushed and smothered.

As the chuckles died away, somebody had a bright idea. 'The ruck lifter! Set it up on wan side o' the stack. Put a rope through the pulley wi' a noose on the end o't. We'll lassoo the wee bugger an' haul him oot.'

We ran to the implement shed and, after some trouble,

manoeuvred the rick lifter out and into position, with the noose dangling above the hole in the stack. But the rope was light. The noose might stick in a narrow part of the shaft. We pulled the whole contraption aside, spreadeagled it and attached a 28-lb. weight to the noose. When the rick lifter was set up again, we were ready.

'Watch oot fur yer heid!' we yelled to the Rat and began lowering the noose.

Down went the weight, sliding and rustling amongst the sheaves.

'Ha'e ye got it?'

'Ay, I've got it.'

'Put the loop ablow yer oxters. We'll heave ye up.... Are ye ready?

'I'm ready!' came a stifled shout.

Four of us at the end of the rope began to pull. And eventually, like a cork being eased out of a bottle, the Rat emerged from the hole, covered with straw, squealing and kicking his legs because of the discomfort of the noose under his armpits.

Danger was past. The stack remained intact. Laughter became permissible again. We thought it a huge joke to keep the Rat dangling for a minute or two.

But finally we let him down and told him to remember to use a straw bag in future. And a tiny piece was added to the mosaic of Southend's folklore.

Working at Dalbhraddan that day, as casual hands, were Big Doser and Kleek. They no longer tried to bully Neil and me; we had grown as tall and strong as they were. In fact, on this occasion we felt a little sorry for them, because in the emergency they had stood open-mouthed and helpless, lacking in either initiative or ideas for rescue. Neil's agility and speed had demonstrated his obvious superiority, and my suggestions had been listened to by Jean's brother with respect. In the end they had obediently taken our orders and the four of us had pulled on the rope together.

I enjoyed harvesting at Dalbhraddan. But not so much as at Brunerican, where Jean, on the death of her mother, had become the lady of the house at fourteen. Even then, when I was only fifteen, we were aware of each other. I hadn't yet asked her to go out with me; but we both knew that this would happen, sooner or later.

In the middle of a harvest afternoon there was always a short break. While the rest of the hands enjoyed tea and 'jeely pieces' in the stackyard, the forkers in the field lay back against piles of sheaves in a mood of comfortable contemplation.

In the high field above Brunerican the scene was worth contemplating. It still is, on a day in September when a wind from the north renders visibility sharp and clear, a photographer's dream.

To the south, the Firth of Clyde spreads out in a blue flood, lapping the coasts of Kintyre and Ayrshire, with Ailsa Craig and Sanda causing the only breaks in a smooth expanse. To the north, beyond the mountains of the Mull of Kintyre, lie Islay's slate-grey hills and the improbable Paps of Jura. To the west, seventeen miles away across the North Channel, are the Antrim hills, with dome-shaped Slimish and Trostan, shaped like a coolie's hat, easily identifiable among them. They engender in us a feeling of romance and mystery, like silhouettes in a Walt Disney cartoon.

The hills of Ireland engender also a feeling of warmth and kinship. Here we are Scots. There they are Irish. But the constant comings and goings across the narrow sea, down through centuries, have blurred the sharp edges of nationality, and in spirit we reach across to one another as loving members of the human race.

We remember that to the people of Ireland we owe an age-old debt. Indeed, we have a common ancestry in the Mesolithic men who crossed from Red Bay to the pier head of the Mull 8000 years ago, and in the tribe of the Scotti who followed them 6000 years later.

Since then they have given us Columba, the saint whose halo, though always a little crooked, still shone with the Spirit. They have given us noble lords with their armourers and *sennachies*. They have given us fishermen and farmers, smugglers, potato-gatherers, thatchers and pedlars of linen goods, whose names and deeds, all of Irish origin, are commemorated in the songs called 'come all ye's' still sung at our local concerts. They have given us an accent subtly different from the mainstream Scots. And today they lend us, for short spells, the Irvines and the MacCambridges, the Spurs and the Kennedys, with whom we can exchange news of Antrim and Kintyre, both ancient and modern, and laugh uproariously at the same kind of jokes.

In those harvest days, sixty years ago, we watched the coastal puffers carrying whisky and coal to and from Glasgow and the Hebridean islands. We watched the great red-funnelled ships belonging to the Anchor Line passing through Sanda Sound, with 'a bone in their teeth', on their way to America.

In place of the liners, we watch the movement of huge oil tankers and container ships, all far out at sea because now they are directed by the Board of Trade to avoid the black-toothed dangers of Sanda. We watch the little grey ships searching for oil in the North Channel and the converted assault craft, also drably grey, carrying supplies to the rocket range in South Uist. We watch black nuclear submarines from the Holy Loch (yes, the *Holy* Loch) near Dunoon going about their ugly business. And in recent times we have watched furtive and sinister vessels carrying nuclear waste from Dounreay to a small, unhappy port in England. Where there was warmth and excitement before, now we experience shivers of apprehension, as if clammy, dead fingers were touching our bodies.

But when I was fifteen, enjoying an afternoon break in the high harvest field, I was less interested in the scenery than in the girl who, leaving the stackyard hands to the ministrations of a serving lass, made it her business to come up to the field alone with a thermos of tea for us and a basket of 'pieces'.

Sometimes Jean and I were able to sit together by ourselves, while the other forkers finished off their 'pieces' behind a distant stook. We looked out across the sparkling sea towards Ireland. We said little; but each of us knew that the other was seeing the Fata Morgana of a life together. This was one Fata Morgana that became, years later, a substantial vision. A vision substantial still.

9. Sportscene

After the First World War, I began to ease myself out of the serpent skin of childhood. The disciplined, protected life at the Manse was never penally irksome (and now I never cease to be grateful for it); but when I came to understand that all things interesting in life were not contained in my native parish and that Southend was not, by any means, the hub of the universe, there was a stirring in my blood and a growing desire for new sensations and new knowledge.

I know that my brother Willie was also dreaming dreams. One day, when he was only ten years old, I saw him sitting on a high branch of the copper beech tree outside the Manse. He had found an old pair of binoculars and was looking through them at the Anchor liner *Transylvania* making passage up the Clyde. In a moment of unusual candour he said to me, 'Some day I'll be captain of a ship like that.' His dream came true. He retired a few years ago as senior skipper with the Anchor Line.

I always wanted to be a writer, and my dream came true as well. It was in outdoor sport, however, that I found most of my recreational pleasures and sensations.

As boys, my friends and I rode dirt track round the Manse avenue on ancient, cannibalized bicycles. The gravel flew; we skidded and crashed into trees, and once, when we attached a go-cart to one of the bicycles and hauled it round after us at speed, with Willie in it (aged five), Maimie the maid screamed terrible Gaelic oaths at us and boxed our ears. '*Chiall beannachd mi!* Would you murder the child!'

We constructed a nine-hole pitch and putt course on the Manse front lawn, imagining the avenue as a river which had to be crossed several times during a round. We began to dig bunkers round some of the greens but were dissuaded from doing so by the awful wrath of my father (and members of the Kirk Session) at such apparent vandalism. But this did not interfere with our pleasure. We assumed the names of Vardon, Braid and Herd – and, as the years went by, of Duncan and Padgham – and played open championships as often as we could arrange them with our pals.

In summer, when we played cricket in the glebe below the Manse, we were Hobbs, Sutcliffe and Strudwick. In winter, playing football, we quarrelled as to which of us should be called Alan Morton.

Thankfully, sixty years on, I can still enjoy my sporting fantasies.

I was there at St Andrews on a sunshine day in July 1978, striding up the last fairway with a two-shot cushion to win the Open. I waved and bowed acknowledgement of the thunderous applause from 15,000 spectators on either side. My name was Jack Nicklaus.

I was there at Moscow in the summer of 1980, running for my life in an outside lane of the 100 metres (from Big Doser and Kleek?) and snatching on the tape the Olympic gold medal. My name was Allan Wells.

From Bobby Kelly, a nephew of Hugh MacEachran, I bought my first real bicycle, as opposed to a home-made one for the dirt track. Or at least my father bought it, for a pound.

I tended it with the care of a twelve-year-old, oiling and greasing and adjusting nuts. I became so expert a rider that I could speed down past the church, pedalling like a maniac without hands. I could also, like my brother Archie, kneel on the saddle and do a flying angel down a steep decline on the Kilblaan side road.

We fell, bruising our limbs; and once, when skidding off the Kilblaan track into a ditch, I sprained my left arm at the elbow. This did not worry me at the time. Now, however, I find it difficult to keep the straight left arm so necessary in a perfect golf swing. But there is a bright side. I am able to exploit my 'disability' as a subtle variant of the many excuses

available to a golfer when he or she mis-hits a shot, confident
in the knowledge that most of my opponents are now too
young to remember – and remind me – that Ed Furgol, who
won the American Open and played for America in the
Ryder Cup, had a withered arm.

When I went to Campbeltown Grammar School – in the
autumn following the visit with my father to North Uist – I
stayed in lodgings in the town from Monday morning until
Friday evening. For three years, week in, week out, my
friend Boskers and I cycled the ten miles to Campbeltown
and the ten miles back. (Boskers will confirm this. He is
otherwise known as Lt. Col. Hamish Taylor, recently con-
venor of Argyll County Council.) We pedalled furiously to
achieve record times, and our fastest, I remember, was
twenty-five minutes, with a brisk north wind in our favour.
But there were other mornings and other evenings, filled
with driving rain, when we took more than an hour to do the
journey.

Eventually 'scholars' buses' were introduced; but by then
Boskers and I, with many hours of hard pedalling behind us,
had developed leg and thigh muscles that were tough and
strong: muscles which stood us in good stead when we began
to take part in the local Highland Games, Boskers as a
shot-putter and hammer-thrower, myself as a sprinter and
jumper. By brute force and a considerable amount of
ignorance I won the Grammar School Sports Championship
two years in succession, and for this I give most of the credit
to my bicycle. (It should be added that the Dux medal for
academic distinction eluded me during the same two years.)

Boskers worked on his father's farm, for, I think, no more
than his keep. I had bursaries to support me at school and,
later, at the university; but my parents, on a ministerial
stipend, had no cash to spare even for occasional doles. Our
problem, therefore, was how to earn enough pocket money
to carry us through the holidays. The Highland Games, with
their money prizes, provided a solution.

We had no coaches, nobody who took the slightest interest
in our leisure pursuits, except our parents in a casual way.
We trained ourselves, using the glebe as a training ground.

With the prize of ten shillings which I won for a first place in the 100 yards at Southend Highland Games (when I was sixteen) I bought a book written by Harold Abrahams, and we followed faithfully all the hints on training for athletics so generously supplied by the Olympic gold medallist.

Eventually we were joined by my brother Archie and his friend, Lachie Young (retired, not long ago, as Director of Education for Perthshire), and by the late Neil John Mac-Callum, a son of the local blacksmith. In time Neil John outshone us all by winning the mile at the most famous of all professional athletic events, the New Year meeting at Powderhall in Edinburgh.

As we grew more confident – and a little more affluent – we toured all the Games in Argyll (Oban, Inveraray, Loch-gilphead, Tayinloan, Campbeltown and Southend), first in an old T-Ford belonging to Boskers' father and then in a bull-nose Morris which I had bought for £7 10s.

Along with our athletic gear we always carried a few sliced potatoes. In those days mechanical wipers had not yet become standard equipment in cars; but when a sliced potato was rubbed against the windscreen its juice dissolved the spots of rain and allowed the driver to see clearly ahead – for a few miles at any rate, until the effect wore off and another quick rub had to be made.

In Southend a minister's son received an excellent ground-ing in the study of human nature. As children we tended to categorize men and women in stark black and white; but when we became adolescents and began to encounter more and more people from alien environments it was brought home to us that the predominant colour in the picture of humanity, like the colour of drapes on a stage, is grey. A grey, nevertheless – again like that of drapes on a stage – which can be the background, under lights, for memorable and sometimes inspiring characters.

Our participation in the games brought us into contact with great sportsmen like Weir of Clydebank and the Andersons of Dundee, who tossed enormous cabers, threw 56-lb. weights over high bars, sent 16-lb. hammers with long wooden shafts hurtling high into the sky and putted heavy

stones (16 lb. and 22 lb.) as if they were marbles. And like
Starkey and McGregor who could jump and pole vault as
well as heave weights about. All were huge men, cool, calm,
rough but entirely honest, who, in the heavy events, invariably competed in their kilts.

One day, at Oban, I sprinted through the tapes at the
finish of a 100-yard race. As recommended by Harold
Abrahams, my head and chest were thrust down at the time,
and I failed to notice that directly in my line of flight stood
George Anderson engaged in smearing a hammer shaft with
a tacky substance which ensured a firm grip. Though I struck
him at speed he remained as immoveable as a tree. I
bounced back off him and landed on my bottom. Momentarily he glanced down at me, with less interest than he would
have shown to a passing bumble bee. 'Get off yer arse!' he
advised me without rancour.

Most of the events were adjudicated by the lairds and the
sons of lairds who inhabited the district in which the Games
were held. Some of them who had been in the army, and had
thereby gained valuable knowledge of piping and Highland
dancing, were excellent judges of those colourful events, and
nobody took advantage of them. But few were expert in the
conduct of athletics.

For example, their preparations for a hurdle race was to
place heavy wooden bars, suspended on three-foot-high
fence stobs, at intervals of about twenty yards around the
circular grass track. At first, as apprentice professionals,
Archie, Lachie and I used to dash off in front and try to jump
those bars. In consequence, we often knocked them down,
bruising our shins and falling on our faces in the process. The
wily old pros dawdled behind us, with the result that they
often had no jumping at all to do and could overtake and
pass the halt and the maimed and the innocent down the
finishing straight.

Sometimes, in the sprints, handicaps were given, each yard
advantage being indicated on the track by wooden pegs with
a line of sawdust or whitewash drawn between them. Here
the scratch men were at a considerable disadvantage. Let me
explain.

As a rule the starter was the product of an English public school where sportsmanship was taught to be among the highest virtues. He would put the scratch man on his mark and then, in a quick gabble, read out our handicaps to the rest of us. 'MacVicar, Angus, three yards. MacVicar, Archibald, five yards. Young, Lachlan, six yards.' And so on. He made no effort to check that we took our proper marks, cheating at sport being something he had been taught to believe impossible.

At our first Games we thought it impossible, too, and advanced carefully to our allotted lines. Then we began to be aware that on the command 'Get to your marks' some of the hard-bitten runners from (to us) mysterious localities like Kilmaurs, Tranent and Galashiels were creeping forward an extra yard or two, without being reprimanded – or even noticed – by the starter. For the unfortunate scratch man, crouching directly under the eyes of the young official, this kind of manoeuvre was impossible.

By hard experience we learned that honesty – particularly in the short races – simply did not pay, and as we were there for the money we played the cheats at their own game and so became cheats ourselves. After a while we suffered no pangs of conscience when taking advantage of innocent newcomers. The trouble is, I now find no pleasure in the memory.

(No doubt some questionable practices still occur at the seventy or eighty Highland and Border Games, which, each year, are held in various parts of the country. Most of these meetings, however, are now conducted under the strict rules of the Scottish Games Association, incorporated in 1946, and I should be surprised if many 'fly' men are allowed to prosper, as we were.)

But good memories of the Games are still available. The skirl of the pipes and the flutter of the kilts and tartan plaids. The neat, tight step of the dancers twirling and turning on high wooden platforms. The scent of mown grass on the running tracks and the sparkle of dew on a sunshine morning. The grunts and triumphant shouts of the heavyweights lifting the cabers high and throwing them over. The spectators moving on the sidelines in streams of changing colours

and their shrieks of applause at the finish of a close race or
for an athlete leaping lithely over the bar of a high jump
stand. And, above all, the smell of embrocation.

Few Highland Games boasted sand pits for the long jump
or for the hop, step and leap. Nor were air cushions provided
for the high jumpers and pole vaulters. We landed heavily on
the turf and, in consequence, were liable to frequent bumps
and bruises. Most of the Games had rubbing tents, where an
athlete whose legs or arms required attention was minstered
to by old professionals. Their active days were over, but they
loved to follow the Games and offer physical comfort and
practical wisdom to those still taking part.

My favourite rubber was Jamie Ma. 'Ma' was obviously a
nickname; I never did discover his real one. He had once
been placed second in the New Year 130-yards sprint at
Powderhall but always maintained that the officials at the
tape were bent, in the pay of the bookmakers, and that he
ought to have won the first prize, which in those days
amounted to the fabulous sum of £100. 'Ma breist hit the
tape first. Maybe the other fella's hand touched it afore I did,
but that was agin the rules.' (If he was telling the truth he
had a point. According to the rules of the Scottish Games
Association 'competitors shall be placed as they strike the
worsted and cross the imaginary line with head, breasts or
legs. Competitors striking the worsted with their hand deliberately may be disqualified at the discretion of the Referee or
Judges.')

Jamie Ma came from an Ayrshire village. He would be in
his late forties when I knew him, about 5 feet 6 inches tall,
stockily built and 'bowly' legged. He worked intermittently
as a coal miner and had the dry cough and blue-pocked face
so often acquired by workers in pre-Coal Board pits. As a
rule he kept his false teeth in a trouser pocket, and I
understood why. With them in his mouth he was so pre-
occupied by keeping them in position that long silences were
broken only by incoherent mumblings. Without them he
spoke clearly – and incessantly.

'Lie doon on the table,' he would tell me. 'On yer belly.'
From a worn and dirty canvas bag he would take a bottle

containing a pungent, white mixture. Pouring some on to his hands he would slap it on my legs and begin a thorough and sometimes painful massage. The smell of his special embrocation was so strong that before he was finished I often found myself in tears.

As he rubbed and then pummelled my thigh and calf muscles with the edges of his hands, he would offer advice and reminiscence in equal quantities, seldom stopping to receive comments from me.

'Ye're ower lang in the leg fur a sprinter. But yer muscles is no' bad. Yer thigh muscles is jeest like ma ain when I was at ma best. Lie still noo 'an let me gi'e them a hammerin'. They're a wee bit tight efter that last race. That's better. . . .

'The first time I ran in the Powderhall sprint I was on the back shift at the pit the nicht before. I hurried hame, but ma mither hadna the breakfast ready, so I had tae dae wi' jeest a cup o' tea. Then wee Sammy Pagan's owld motor broke doon somewhere ootside Edinburgh. I was late reachin' the stadium and hadna time tae get a rub. Haufway doon the track I seized up like Wee Sammy's bloody motor an' I was near last.

'Hooan'ever, that meant that next year I got a guid handicap, eicht yairds. I took bloody guid care that this time I was at the stadium early, an' Wee Sammy basted an' bashed me like a turkey, usin' the same stuff as I'm usin' on yersel'. It's a secret recipe, ye ken, invented by Wee Sammy's faither, who was a sprinter tae. I should ha'e won that day – Wee Sammy had a packet on me – but thae buggers at the tape were nobbled by the bookies an' I lost ma chance. Wee Sammy couldna afford a drink fur weeks efter't. An' neither could I. . . .

'But ach, some o' the sprinters is as bad as the offeecials. See yon big bugger frae Glesca wi' the fair hair an' the broon skin. Ye'd think he was a hauf-cast, but he's no'. Sun-ray treatment – that's why his skin's sae broon. His faither runs a gym an' a Turkish bath fur Glesca business men. Watch him on the bends, son. He'll cut across ye in the fower-forty if he gets the chance, an' it'll no worry him if he spikes ye forbye. Listen. If he comes on yer ootside on the last bend, dae whit I used tae dae. Let on ye've been tripped frae behin', fling oot yer richt airm as if tae steady yersel' an' hit him hard in the stomach. Ye'll be at the tape afore he gets his win' back....

'Noo then, hoo dae ye feel? ... That's gran'. Away oot there an' mak' me proud o' ye. I'm no' backin' ye fur the hunner yairds: yon wee nyaff frae Tranent's far quicker aff his mark as ye'll ever be. But I've a pound on ye fur the two-twenty. Wi' thae lang legs o' yours nane o' them should see ye fur dust doon the feenishin' straight. No' even the big bugger frae Glesca. Wad ye like me tae putt a pound on fur yersel'?'

This, of course, was the business end of our one-sided conversation. His usual charge for a rub was a pound. Now he was suggesting, in as friendly a way as possible, that I should give him two pounds. He knew that I knew that he had no intention of risking even a ha'penny on the off-chance of my winning the two-twenty.

But I always gave him the two pounds. One way and another I felt he had earned them.

On the way home from the Inveraray Highland Games, having won a fair amount of money between us, Archie and Lachie and Boskers and I always used to stop for a slap-up high tea at Lochgair Hotel, north of Lochgilphead. Mine host was John Sinclair, who was married to a MacVicar lady, a far-out relative of my own. John's hotel was well known throughout Scotland for real Highland hospitality.

First of all, as we sat down with mouth-watering appetites after a day's hard work in the open air, our table was supplied with home-baked scones, pancakes, cream sponge cake, shortbread, and gingerbread. Then came the teacups and the plates, the cream jugs and the sugar bowls, dishes of real butter and a squat glass jar containing some of Mrs Sinclair's special rhubarb jam. Then the toast, a laden rack for each of us. Then the tea in two huge silver pots, flanked by another silver pot of hot water. And finally an ashet (a Scots word for a large – in this case *very* large – flat dish), piled high with sizzling rashers of bacon and at least a dozen fried eggs, from which we could help ourselves.

At this point, round and smiling and sparing of words,

jacketless and with a silver watch chain draped across his bulging waistcoat, John Sinclair would come into the dining-room, ask how we had got on at the Games and then retire to a position near the doorway, where he could watch us eat. As the ashet was emptied, as the scones and the cakes and the sponges disappeared, his smile would grow broader. When the teapots and the hot-water jug had been drained and only crumbs were left on the plates he would approach us again and ask if we wanted more. We never did. We were full to bursting point. But in our awkward way we would indicate our appreciation of a marvellous meal.

He would shake his bald head. 'You've thanked me already,' he'd say. And once he added, 'The MacCrimmons didna mak pipe tunes for the money. They made them for the folk tae enjoy.'

At the time, as a beginning writer, I understood vaguely what he meant. Now I understand exactly what he meant. I still wait, with halting breath, not only for the cash my books bring in but also for the reactions of readers and critics. When I receive a letter of appreciation from a stranger or a favourable review in a national newspaper, my smile becomes as broad as John Sinclair's. Royalty cheques keep an author's body alive; but it is proven success in giving pleasure to others that nurtures his spirit.

Incidentally, I remember that for one of his famous high teas John Sinclair charged 3s. 6d.

When I took an active part in athletics, more than fifty years ago, professional runners and jumpers had a bad image. They were known as 'peds' (in the *Glasgow Herald* their doings were always recorded under the heading of 'Pedes-trianism'), and high-minded amateurs would describe them as money-grubbers always prepared to cheat and steal for the sake of an odd sixpence. This description was true in some cases. But in the 1920s and 1930s, when social security was embryonic, a poor man simply could not afford to run except for money. And there were as many honest sports-men among the professionals as among the amateurs. I know this to be true because I have run races in both categories.

And I may add that it was an amateur whose spikes caused the livid scar which decorates the inside of my left calf. (A scar which I am happy to unveil at the slightest sign of interest.)

In my young days, however, the main sponsors of many a promising young athlete were the bookmakers. As a result he often became caught up in a financial quagmire. This consisted of loans which tied him to a certain 'school', of subsidies to cover the expense of secret training, of small bribes to run poorly at certain games in order to acquire a favourable mark later in the season. If he failed to win on a certain specified occasion and thereby make a killing for his backers, he was liable to be tossed aside like an old dishcloth and left to fend for himself.

Without the support of the system this was no easy task. Archie, Lachie, Neil John and I were able to do so for a time. But in the end, refusing all offers from sly-eyed strangers, we found ourselves being handicapped so severely that the only kind of race we had any chance of winning was one in which all the competitors started from scratch. And even then it was curious how often we were knocked off our stride, early in the race, by somebody banging into us.

I suppose part of the trouble was that none of us had the talent and the courage of Eric Liddell, the greatest runner Scotland had ever produced, amateur or professional, until Allan Wells came on the scene more than half a century later.

Eric Liddell's parents were both missionaries in North China, where he was born in 1902, in Tientsin. He came to study in Edinburgh, where his athletic potential was soon recognized. A fellow student made a joke about him in the university magazine. 'Eric's early days,' he wrote, 'were spent happily chasing Chinese whippets or running against streaks of lightning, while the little Chinese boys and girls sat and held their breaths, astounded.'

At the university he worked hard, training for his chosen profession as a medical missionary. He won a rugby blue and played left wing threequarter for Scotland. But it was as a sprinter that he made his reputation.

He became my hero on a day in July 1923, when, at Stoke-on-Trent, he ran for Scotland against England and Ireland. That day he won not only the 100 and the 220 yards but also the 440 yards. And what a race that 440 was.

In the first three strides, Gillis of England knocked into him. Eric stumbled and almost fell. For the fraction of a second he seemed ready to give up. But then, suddenly, he was going after them — twenty yards behind but still going after them.

As they reached the home straight he was running fourth. Forty yards from the tape he was third, ten yards behind Gillis. He looked exhausted, pale, on the point of collapse. But he pulled himself together once again and in a desperate finish won the race by about a yard, with Gillis second.

On the track beyond the tape he fell and, for a time, lay unconscious.

Even for money, Archie, Lachie and I were not prepared to rack our bodies to such an extent, though it is possible we had the physical strength to do it. Eric Liddell did it for nothing, which shows how far his spirit soared above ours.

Incredible as it may seem today, some English sports writers had been saying he was scarcely good enough for the 1924 Olympic Games. (Perhaps not so incredible: fifty-seven years later, from their journalistic ivory towers, they were saying the same about Allan Wells.) His performance at Stoke-on-Trent, however, caused them to reconsider their judgement. He was chosen to run in Paris in all the sprints, though his own personal sights were set on the 100 metres.

When the lists were published it was revealed that the heats of the 100 metres were to be run on a Sunday. Eric said, firmly, 'In that case I'm not running. Not in the 100 metres at any rate.'

His decision was based on a principle which may now seem outdated and even illogical; but he never wavered. Afterwards he had no regrets, not even when the 100 metres was won by Harold Abrahams, a man he had already beaten, several times.

So now it was the 400 metres or nothing. (He had won a bronze medal in the 200 metres, but he considered his running in that race to have been 'unsatisfactory'.)

The favourite in the 400 metres final was the great American, H. M. Fitch, who had recorded the best time in the heats. Not only that. In 1924 there was no running in lanes, with staggered starts, and E. H. Liddell was drawn on the outside.

Just before the race started, while Eric was limbering up, an unknown man in the crowd called him over and handed him a piece of paper. As he stood there, looking at some writing on it, he was called to his mark with the others.

The pistol went. Fitch was off in front, streaking for the bend. But then, in the back straight, a white-vested figure was seen to be pounding at Fitch's heels: a chunky, powerful figure, arms flailing, head thrown back. It was Eric Liddell, the man so many had reckoned to have no chance at the Olympic Games because of his ungainly style.

As he rounded the bend into the finishing straight he was on Fitch's shoulder. And at this moment Fitch seemed to recognize that he was beaten. In front of a shouting, screaming crowd in the Colombes Stadium Eric passed him easily and broke the tape with six yards to spare. His time was 47.6 seconds, which was then an Olympic record.

Later in the same year a graduation ceremony took place at Edinburgh University. From a ruck of many names one was called: Eric Henry Liddell, Bachelor of Science. The audience rose to their feet. The building shook with their applause.

'Mr Liddell,' said the Vice-Chancellor, 'you have shown that no man can pass you but the examiner. In the name of the University, which is proud of you, I present you with this scroll and place upon your head this chaplet of wild olives.'

Afterwards, the students carried their champion shoulder high to the steps of St Giles Cathedral, where the citizens of Edinburgh let their hair down and accorded him a welcome far louder and more fervent than that given, forty years later, to the Beatles.

And the underlying cause of such a day of glory? I do not think it was altogether the fact of Eric Liddell's physical strength and courage. A clue may be found in thé piece of paper put into his hand in the tense seconds before he ran the race of his life in Paris. Before he died in a Shantung Internment camp in 1946, he himself told a friend what was written on it. A text from I Samuel: 'These that honour me I will honour.'

That the character and reputation of an athlete should be judged on his standing either as an amateur or a professional has always seemed to me to be ridiculous. It has always been the case that if a person runs or jumps against a professional, whether for a money prize or not, then that person automatically receives a black ball and is branded professional, unfit to stride the track with the Eric Liddells, the Allan Wellses and the Linsey MacDonalds of this world. And to be reinstated as an amateur costs money and time and worry, none of which a young man or woman can easily afford.

Even in cricket, which I imagine to be a game of the utmost conservatism, Gentleman have regularly competed against Players. In golf, Bobby Jones, an amateur, played continually against the professionals, frequently beating them, but with never a complaint from anyone. (In one year, 1930, he won what has been called 'The Impregnable Quadrilateral': the Open Championship, the American Open Championship, the British Amateur Championship and the American Amateur Championship.) In football, the amateur club, Queen's Park, is welcomed in the professional leagues. Nowadays, in tennis, important tournaments like that at Wimbledon are all open to amateurs and professionals. It is the same with every other major sport, except athletics. (And, in a peculiarly archaic sense, rugby.)

I could never and still cannot understand why a man or woman who possesses talent as an athlete should become the subject of denigration, denied all the benefits of official support, simply because he or she can only afford to develop it by accepting money prizes. Somebody with a talent for music can play for money in an orchestra and still be regarded as a lady or a gentleman. Somebody with a talent for painting can sell canvases in a back alley and still aspire to the Royal Academy. Somebody with a talent for writing has always to endure competition from hordes of eager amateurs but is not looked upon with disfavour because he or she becomes a professional in self-defence.

In my youth I ran at the Glasgow University Sports as well as at the Highland Games and won several medals. Archie and Lachie did the same. But then somebody informed the authorities that we were, in effect, professionals, which involved us in an interrogation as ruthless, it seemed to me, as the Inquisition. Archie and Lachie applied successfully for reinstatement as amateurs, and eventually Archie won a soccer blue, which might have been denied him had he remained a professional athlete. I did not apply for reinstatement. I continued to run at the Highland Games and, though invited to return them, kept my amateur medals. I still have those medals in a box. I am proud of them. If the university or the SAAA want them back they will have to come and get them.

Surely it is time that athletics was made an open sport, like the others. Not only would it encourage young people to achieve a high standard of physical fitness and self-discipline; it would also stifle the hypocrisy which at present grows like lichen on the rules and regulations of the governing bodies.

Most of the men and women famous in athletics today are sponsored, in much the same way as the old peds were. They receive hidden expenses. They are employed by firms which give them unlimited time off. They are trained by professional coaches who are, in effect, civil servants. Every now and then a bright newspaper reporter unearths a scandal, which suggests that some notable amateur has been paid expenses far exceeding those allowed by the rules. This causes no more than a ripple on the turgid surface of the sport, because all concerned – especially the influential firms which sponsor important athletic meetings as part of their advertising campaigns – would lose a great deal of money and credibility if the inquiry were pursued to its logical conclusion. If athletes were paid openly for their skills, the organization of many an unsavoury cover-up would no longer be necessary.

I find it significant that it is the so-called purely amateur sports which often become involved in the hypocritical dealings of certain politicians.

In the midst of all this confusion of moral values – the trade mark of a dying century – I look back at my careless youth with envy. My ideals then were bright, impervious, I believed, to tarnish. The Padre taught us that life was simple and direct, a matter of good versus evil, with the good, like the US cavalry, charging in to victory at the end. I think differently now. Good does not always triumph, as TV playwrights keep reminding us, *ad nauseam*. Politicians, public relations officers and advertising agents have become highly skilled in the art of portraying evil as good. My ageing brain keeps telling me that standards do not change and that the Ten Commandments are always there, a spiritual lifebelt. But the seas are choppy, and sometimes I find difficulty in grabbing hold of it, especially when some modern apologist tugs at the line and tries to snatch it away from me.

I try to believe I am still the boy I was and find a certain comfort in the words of Shakespeare: 'You that are old consider not the capacities of us that are young: you measure the heat of our livers with the bitterness of your galls: and we that are in the vaward of our youth, I must confess, are wags, too.'

10. The Power of a Rose

This book is my first attempt at a real autobiography. In order to answer the question 'Why am I what I am?', I looked back on my childhood and tried to describe some of the influences, both human and environmental, which surrounded me more than half a century ago. But it soon became evident – to me, at any rate – that I should have to probe further, especially into the influences which had involved my father as a boy in North Uist. And when I did that, an urge came on me to dig even deeper into the past, first into the history of the MacVicar priests of the thirteenth century and then down and down into Scottish history.

I realize now, however, that all such devoted research has been largely an exercise in self-indulgence and that, once again, as a writer of autobiography I have failed. I went digging in dark peat mosses, endeavouring to prove a theory that heredity plays an important part in our personalities. Interesting artefacts were uncovered: but it seems to me that I found nothing of satisfying substance. My original question has been answered only superficially. Perhaps grains of truth have glinted momentarily in the debris, including some which I now find myself wishing had not been revealed.

Was the question worth asking in the first place? My life, my knowledge, my prejudices, are they of any importance whatsoever in a world teeming with so many million neighbours? I try to believe that my efforts to find an answer may be of some infinitesimal value in that they demonstrate that I love my neighbours – most of them, at any rate – and find happiness in recording it.

The writing of this book, too, has given me a clearer picture of the changes that have taken place in society, both material and spiritual, in the past sixty or seventy years.

Material changes have been many in Southend at the Mull of Kintyre: changes which reflect similar ones in rural communities everywhere.

In his song, Paul McCartney refers to Southend as consisting of mountains and heather, with 'mist rolling in from the sea'. The description comes mainly from Paul's romantic imagination.

In my childhood, before the development of marketing boards and social services, it shared government neglect and consequent poverty with other remote Scottish parishes. Today it is a busy and, on the whole, prosperous farming area, with undulating acres of fertile land sheltered by the mountains. Its population includes not only farmers and farm workers but also fishermen, shipyard workers, business people young and old (who commute to offices in Campbeltown), shopkeepers, hotelkeepers and a number of senior citizens who, having retired to an imagined haven of peace and quiet, now find themselves constantly active as they become involved in the kirk, in guilds, in rurals, in drama and in golf. For the young in body and heart there is a badminton club and a football club and parties and discos galore arranged by the community council. At times mist does roll in from the sea, though rain and howling gales are much more frequent. In general, however, the climate is mild (thanks, it would appear, to the proximity of the Gulf Stream) and Jean and I can harvest vegetables from our garden, without the aid of a greenhouse, as early as they can in the Channel Islands.

There is one example of material change in Southend which may serve as an example of what has been happening in my day and age.

Here, as I sit at my writing table, I look out of the window and see, beyond Dunaverty Rock, the island of Sanda, separated from the coast by two miles of water. Today the only people who live there are the on duty lighthouse-keepers, whose families and permanent homes are in Campbeltown. It has a fine sheltered harbour, a fact appreciated by the Vikings, who in the dark centuries between the time of St Columba and that of Robert the Bruce, used it əs a rallying place for their invasion fleets. On old maps the island is sometimes called Avon, no doubt from the Norse word meaning 'haven'.

In the Middle Ages Sanda became an important religious centre. St Ninian's chapel, the ruins of which, situated above the harbour, are still fairly well preserved, was included in Fordun's list of ecclesiastical foundations in the Western Isles of Scotland, compiled during the second half of the fourteenth century. It also used to support a small farming and fishing community. Now the fields and farmhouse have become almost derelict.

The old chapel and graveyard are of considerable interest to archaeologists. An old man in Southend, whose father had been born in Sanda, once took me across in his boat and showed me his family burial ground. Near it lay an ancient flagstone about which he told me a strange story. In olden times, he said, when the crew of a boat were in danger at sea, people ashore used to gather round the stone, wash it with clean water and chant an incantation beseeching the person buried below to have mercy on those in danger.

'Who is buried below?' I asked.

'Nobody knows. But I can repeat the incantation, if you like.'

It was in the Gaelic, of course; but here is a rough translation:

> Champion famed for warlike toil
> Art thou silent, mighty?
> I come not with unhallowed dread
> To wake the slumbers of the dead.
> Waken now or sleep for ever,
> For thus the sea
> Shall smooth its ruffled crest for thee,
> And, while afar its billows foam,
> Subside the peace near Halcc's Tomb.

Once again the Norse connection?

Sanda used to belong to the Clan Donald; but as the centuries passed it fell into the hands of various owners. In

1929, when agricultural conditions were poor, it was purchased by the tenant farmer, Sandy Russell, for £900. (This figure and those which follow are, of course, approximate.)

Sandy Russell was successful as a farmer, even though the conveyance of his sheep and cattle to the mainland markets was often an awkward and sometimes even dangerous business. His son, Jim, was successful too. And when the latter retired to live in Southend in 1969, the island was bought by Jack Bruce, guitarist in the pop group called the Cream, for £35,000.

For the next few years Jack Bruce and his family came to the island as often as they could, living in the farmhouse. He composed a great deal of music while in Sanda, and a television film was made of his life there.

Eventually, however, he grew tired of his island hideaway, and in 1976 he sold it to James Gulliver, the well-known financier, for £75,000.

Though James Gulliver is a Campbeltown man – his father had a grocer's shop there, and he himself attended the local grammar school – he soon found that Sanda did not suit his family needs as a holiday resort. In 1979 he disposed of it to a gentleman reputed to be an Iranian for £125,000. We have never seen the new owner but he is known to us as Mr Chengezi.

Not long before this transaction took place, it had been confidently predicted by a member of the Coal Board that oil would be found in plenty below the nearby waters of the North Channel. Is it possible that in the near future great fleets will again sail into Sanda harbour – fleets not of Viking longships but of giant tankers?

In a spiritual sense, Southend is lucky in that it has been able to retain its identity as a community. This, I believe, is mainly due to its having the sea on three sides and only one good road leading out of it. A feeling of neighbourliness persists, which may be due to the fact that everybody in the parish knows what everybody else is doing – and even thinking. The ground is unfertile for public relations officers who manipulate public images and for media propagandists who preach a creed sometimes called 'liberal' but which, in effect, undermines all respect for the dignity of the individual.

For me, the cult of the anti-hero signposts a considerable change which, in my lifetime, has taken place in the mores of our society. Why is it so assiduously promoted in books, in newspapers, and on radio and television? Is it because of awareness on the part of writers and producers that in such characters we see our mirror images and can thereby side-step guilt by persuading ourselves that the whole human race is as weak and undisciplined as we are? ('Pap for the masses'?)

My generation was encouraged to have heroes and heroines. St Columba, Robert the Bruce, Joan of Arc, Lady Grizel Baillie, Eric Liddell, Barney Ross, Odette, Ben Hogan: these are but a few. They struggled, they faced hardship and disappointment, but ultimately gained a victory, not only for themselves but also for mankind.

I cannot understand why the young of today should be encouraged to admire instead – for example – amoral train robbers, Wimbledon wailers, drug-addicted pop stars and, in fiction, drunken, womanizing detectives and grotty cowboys with all the graces of barracudas. No wonder society appears to be uncaring, when loving one's neighbour is so often represented as a sign of 'wetness'. It is valid, of course, to record the doings of such unlovely people; but it is equally valid – and, in my opinion, more valuable – to record the deeds of the heroes and heroines. Because, in the end, there can be no happiness without love. Christ, the ultimate hero, died to prove it. Hitler, the ultimate anti-hero, died to prove that hate means death and destruction. And oblivion.

I suppose that something of my character is revealed in that three of the heroes on my list are sportsmen. Two of them happen to be American, one a boxer, the other a golfer.

Barney Ross's real name was Rosofsky. His father was a smalltime grocer in a Chicago slum. One day gangsters called at the shop and demanded protection money. When Rosofsky senior tried to argue they shot him dead.

Barney was only fourteen, but the family now became his

responsibility. He sold papers and worked as a shoeshine boy, all the time making Walter Mitty plans to better the family fortunes.

In due course, one of his plans came true. In 1928, as an amateur, he won a Golden Gloves title in New York. Despite his mother's disapproval, he changed his name to Ross and became a professional boxer.

Money – real money – began to come in, but his mother refused to give his new way of life her blessing. Never, she said, would she go and see him fight.

When he was twenty-five, Barney took on Tony Canzoneri for the lightweight championship of the world. After half a dozen rounds there was little between them, as far as boxing skill was concerned. In the seventh Barney seemed to be getting the worst of it, when suddenly a woman began screaming encouragement from the ringside. He glanced down through the ropes and saw his mother. After that, as one commentator wrote, 'Canzoneri was a dead duck'.

But one world championship was not enough for Barney. Or for his mother, who now realized that her son had the stability of character to be rich and famous and yet remain unspoilt.

Before a crowd of 45,000, he won the welterweight title from Jimmy McLarnin, though some of the crowd thought the referee had given the wrong verdict. But the referee's name was Jack Dempsey, and Jack Dempsey, ex-heavyweight champion of the world, could scarcely be called inexperienced.

Barney Ross retired from boxing just before the Second World War, with what a journalist on the *Washington Post* called 'an unsurpassed record of sportsmanship and gallantry'. He was over thirty now, but he volunteered for the Marines. At Gaudalcanal he won the Distinguished Service Cross for an action in which he saved three wounded comrades by holding a slit-trench single-handed against repeated attack by the Japanese.

He himself was wounded in this fight and taken to hospital, where the doctors relieved his headaches with a certain drug – an experimental drug which seemed to be effective at the time. But after the war Barney's headaches recurred. He began using the drug again, on his own account. Before he could understand what was happening, he had become an addict.

His marriage and his health broke down. He became a pathetic Skid Row figure, bleary-eyed, always searching for new supplies of the stuff that was killing him.

In his brain, however, a spark of moral sense remained alight. One day in September 1946, it flared up, stronger than usual. He stumbled into his lawyer's office in Manhattan, his clothing ragged, his hands trembling. 'I'm sick,' he muttered, with desperate humility. 'My wife has left me, and I'm ready to be counted out. Please – please help!'

Those of us who, by good fortune, have never known the spirit-sapping effect of drugs can scarcely comprehend the courage it took to make this plea. But Barney Ross was committed now. The fight was on, in the public health service hospital in Lexington, Kentucky: a fight to a sad and painful finish, according to the pessimists and the worldly wise.

But this is not a modern scenario, with a down-beat curtain. This is true. Months later a New York newspaper came out with a banner headline: 'Barney Ross KO's Drug Habit'. The champion had won his last great fight.

He left hospital cured, began courting his wife again and eventually remarried her.

A happy ending, old-fashioned, corny. Strange how the brave and battered human spirit quite often supplies one.

And Ben Hogan. Why is Ben Hogan another of my heroes?

When he came to play in the Open Golf Championship at Carnoustie in 1953 I was hoping fervently that he would be beaten by British players. At the time I knew nothing of his story.

He was born in 1912, in Dublin, Texas, a small cattle town about 75 miles from Fort Worth. His father, the town blacksmith and junk dealer, died when Ben was only nine years old, and the family, consisting of his mother, a brother, a sister and himself, moved to Fort Worth. Like Barney Ross, he worked hard, selling newspapers. Eventually he became a caddie at Fort Worth's Glen Garden Country Club.

In 1932 he began to play golf for a living, at first without conspicuous success. Two years later he married Valerie Fox, a girl he had met at Sunday school in Dublin when he was twelve. Jimmy Demaret, another distinguished American golfer, wrote of her: 'Valerie is a girl blessed with strong insight and sure knowledge of what her husband needs from her. In my opinion she has been one of his secret weapons, as fine a woman as it has been my privilege to meet.'

In spite of his wife's encouragement, however, Hogan's golf was still not good enough to win important tournaments. When he came to play at Oakland, California, in late February 1937, he had only five dollars in his pocket. For a time he and Valerie had been living on hamburgers; now the money even for these was running out. 'If I don't win here,' Ben told his wife, 'we'll sell the car and go home. I'll try to get a steady job.'

He played reasonably well for the first two days of the tournament, remaining in contention for a good prize; but his putting worried him so much that he stayed awake for most of the night before the final day. In the morning, when he and Valerie went to collect their car (which they had left in a vacant lot because they could not afford the fee for the main car park), they found it resting on its steel rims. Somebody had jacked it up and stolen the four tyres.

'I felt sick,' Ben said later. 'I thought for sure it was the end. How could I even get to the golf course?'

It was then than Valerie took charge. 'Don't be silly,' she said. 'We'll ride out to the course with somebody else. Don't get upset about it.'

They were given a lift by one of the other competitors, and that day Ben played his heart out. He finished the fourth round to make a total score of 280, good enough for a tie for sixth place. And, more important, a prize of 380 dollars. That evening there were hamburgers galore for himself and Valerie. And new tyres for the car.

The money he won at Oakland was enough to keep Hogan going on the tournament trail, for a few weeks at any rate.

But still the important prizes – the winner's prizes – eluded him.

Towards the end of the 1937 winter season, Henry Picard, then professional at Hershey, Pennsylvania, and a big money winner on the tour, was staying at the Blackstone Hotel at Fort Worth. One evening, in the corner of the lobby, he spotted Ben Hogan and Valerie, whom he had met earlier in the year during an event at Hershey. The pair seemed to be arguing.

Picard went across. 'What's the matter?' he said.

Ben replied with his usual frankness. 'I don't have enough money for both of us to make the tour, and I'm not going alone. Val wants me to go without her, but I won't do it. I'm giving up.'

Valerie, however, continued to argue. 'You can't give up the game, Ben. Not now, after all you've been through.'

Picard was a wealthy man. He was a kind and good man. He was a golfer. To him the answer to their problem was simple. 'All right,' he said. 'Let's end the argument. Ben, take Valerie with you and go out and play. If you need anything, come and see me. I'll take care of things.'

The conversation was casual. It lasted less than ten minutes. But, according to Ben himself, it saved him for golf. From that day he began to earn a steady income from the tournaments, with plenty of small luxuries for Valerie. At the end of the 1939 tour, when Henry Picard decided to accept an offer from Cleveland's Canterbury Club, Hogan was appointed professional at Hershey, which gave him a solid base from which he could work. In 1940, at Pinehurst, North Carolina, he won the North and South Open with a score of 277, a record for the event. At last he had arrived.

By the time he came to Carnoustie, thirteen years later, he had won almost every important tournament in America, including four US Opens.

In his book, *My Partner Ben Hogan*, published in 1954, Jimmy Demaret recounts a conversation he once had with Henry Picard. 'Ben and I hardly know each other, even today,' Picard told him, 'but he dedicated his book to me, and I know we are close friends. I'm the most surprised person in the world that what I said that day in the Blackstone Hotel meant so much to him. And the funniest angle of all is that I never loaned Ben a penny. He never asked for it. All I did was promise to back him up. I could see he was a fine player. It would have been a shame if he had left golf; he has been such a credit to the game.'

A little love, a little care. For Ben Hogan it worked wonders. And I like the style of Henry Picard.

After spending three frustrating years in the Army Air Corps during the Second World War, while Byron Nelson, excused national service because of a tendency to haemophilia, was ruling the American golf scene with a Midas touch, Ben returned to play in tournaments at the end of 1945. He made up for lost time by taking first place in thirteen consecutive events. In 1948 he won his first Open at the Riviera Country Club at Los Angeles. A local newspaper renamed the course 'Hogan's Alley'.

But for all his success, fate held in store for him a terrible reckoning.

On 2 February 1949, he and Valerie were on their way to inspect a new house they had bought in Fort Worth, after he had taken part in the Arizona Open. A heavy fog overlay the highway which crosses the West Texan plain. Two hundred miles from El Paso, at a place called Van Horne, Ben was carefully picking his way through the mirk at ten miles an hour. He saw the headlights of a truck approaching in the opposite lane. Then the two headlights suddenly became four as a huge Greyhound bus swerved out to pass the truck. It came thundering straight at the Hogans' Cadillac.

To Ben's right there was a deep culvert. He had no chance of avoiding a head-on collision. At the last moment he let go of the wheel and threw himself in front of Valerie, an action which saved her life – and, as it happened, his own. As the bus struck with a rending crash, the wheel of the Cadillac was hammered back, burying itself in the driving seat from which Ben had flung himself sideways a moment before. The truck jammed on its brakes and slithered sideways on the road. Another car ran into it. In the blinding fog a fifth vehicle slammed into the tangled wreckage.

Four hours after the accident Hogan was admitted to the Hotel Dieu, a hospital at El Paso. His pelvis was fractured. His left collar bone, left ankle and several ribs were broken. The doctors gave him only an outside chance of survival.

But he survived, with Valerie constantly at his bedside, willing him to live. The physical fitness he had acquired in his years as a professional golfer overcame the shock and the pain and the broken bones. On his third day at the hospital they encased him in a plaster cast from his chest to his knees and put another on his ankle. He smiled wryly. 'Now I'll beat this thing,' he told his wife. 'I'll be back playing golf real soon.'

She believed him; but the doctors didn't. The doctors were mistaken.

In three months from the date of the accident Hogan was out of hospital. With grim determination he began to learn how to walk again. Step by uncertain step he built up his strength. Then he began, stiffly, to play a little golf: pitching and putting first, finally long irons and drives. Day after day he practised. His body was often full of pain; but it also became iron hard. His hands were calloused; but his swing was back, his spirit recharged.

In January 1950, he tied with Sam Snead for the Los Angeles Open. He lost the play-off, because, in the words of Grantland Rice, the sportswriter, 'his legs weren't strong enough to carry his heart around'. But he was happy. And so was Valerie. The Hawk, as he was nicknamed now, was back in business. Indeed, that same year he won the US Open for the second time.

When he came to Scotland to play in the Open, tales of his mechanical golf and dour, unrelenting character preceded him. For some reason, however, few British golf writers enlarged upon the dramatic details which revealed the truth about his life. Jean and I, with our son Jock, then sixteen years old and unaware that the next time the Open was played at Carnoustie he would be reporting it for the *Daily Express*, were among thousands of spectators who hoped to see this arrogant American humbled.

When I saw Hogan for the first time I was surprised by

how small and frail he looked. I could even detect the traces
of a limp as he walked. But there was nothing frail about the
iron shots he struck, long and straight, towards his caddie,
Cecil Timms, on the practice ground. And strangely, when I
saw the face under the white cap, grey, gaunt and expression-
less, the feeling it gave me was not one of antagonism but
rather of sympathy. On one occasion, as I watched him
complete a practice round, Valerie was pointed out to me
among the crowd behind the eighteenth green. It occurred to
me that if he could retain the love and devotion of such a
beautiful woman there must be more to Hogan than
appeared on the surface.

In the two qualifying rounds – though he had no difficulty
in qualifying – Hogan played poorly by his own standards.
On the opening round of the championship proper he scored
a 73, three shots behind the American amateur, Frank
Stranahan, who led the field. By this time, piece by piece and
from various sources, I was learning the Hogan story, and my
heart, albeit reluctantly, was warming towards this small
quiet stranger with the steadfast eyes.

Jock's hero at the time was Dai Rees. Jean had taken a
fancy to a young Australian with a quick smile and white
shoes, who was competing in the Open for the first time: his
name, Peter Thomson. As usual I was hoping that John
Panton and Eric Brown would do well. In those days
spectators were allowed on the course, and we were able to
walk immediately behind our favourites or to sit beside some
green and watch them playing through.

At the end of the second day Jock and I were overjoyed.
Stranahan had stumbled with a 74. Dai Rees and Eric Brown
were tied for the lead on 142. But we noted with interest that
Hogan, finishing with a 71, was only two shots behind them.
And we had discovered that beneath the grim exterior there
was humour. To a fellow professional he had remarked, 'I
understand the tees we are using here are called 'tiger' tees. I
believe it. They are so far back among the heather and gorse
that every time I drive I expect a tiger to jump out at me.'

The last day was cloudy, with squally showers. This meant
that Jean and Jock and I did a lot of walking, because if we

sat down for any length of time we felt cold and uncomfortable. We weren't surprised that Hogan played both rounds with two sweaters on top of his favourite turtle-necked pullover. What we didn't know was that he had contracted flu and spent a restless night with pains in his back. Indeed, he and Valerie told nobody about his physical condition until after the championship was over.

An added interest for us was that for his two final rounds Hogan was paired with Hector Thomson, whom we knew personally. (Ex-Amateur Champion, Hector is one of the famous golfing family of Thomsons from Machrihanish in Kintyre.) We forgot the cold and the occasional rain as we joined the crowd that followed them.

In the morning Hogan scored 70, which included a double bogey 6 on the seventeenth hole, where, after driving into a bunker, he took three putts on the green. In the afternoon he went round in 68, a record for the course, and became Open Champion. His total score of 282 beat by eight strokes the previous competitive best over Carnoustie.

I think a shot we saw him play at the fifth hole that afternoon was the one that inspired his victory. His second to the sloping green rolled back almost into a bunker. The ball was on a sandy lie, fifty feet from the pin. Using a seven-iron – I *think* – he chipped it straight into the hole for a birdie. He was shivering with flu, he had a stiff and painful back, and yet his self-control was so marvellous that he could execute to perfection the most difficult shot in golf – a short pitch off sandy turf.

I remember two interviews which appeared in a magazine after the Carnoustie Open.

One was with Hector Thomson. He had been asked about Hogan's apparent coldness. 'Why, for example,' asked the interviewer, 'did he seem so indifferent when the spectators were cheering him on?'

'He was anything but indifferent,' Hector answered. 'Every time they applauded one of his shots he'd murmur 'Thank you'. You had to be close to hear it, but it was always there.' Then he added, 'He's a fine sportsman as well as a great golfer.'

Hector should know. He is also a fine sportsman and a great golfer.

The other interview was with Hogan himself. He was neither a hypocrite nor in any way sanctimonious, yet he concluded it by saying, 'I don't think anybody does anything unless the Lord's with them. I think the Lord has let me win so many tournaments for a purpose. I hope that purpose is to give courage to all those people who are sick or injured and broken in body as I once was.'

'Intellectuals' among the media men insist that what the public should read and hear and see are slices of real life. Hands on anguished hearts, they thrust such slices at us, brilliantly depicting cruelty, sadism, selfishness, social deprivation and tragedy, everything including the kitchen sink. They have a right to do so, of course. My worry is that they would sneer at the two stories I have just told about Barney Ross and Ben Hogan and dismiss them as being beyond the pale of 'real art', simply because they tell also of courage, integrity and the triumph of the human spirit. The slices of real life which have become fashionable (though not, I believe, with the majority of readers, listeners and viewers) are true. But then are not the stories of Barney Ross and Ben Hogan, with their elements of social deprivation and tragedy, also true? A further question arises. Which are more balanced?

Old Mary MacAulay saw a fairy city in the sky. Are the media men afraid to recognize a Fata Morgana, noble and beautiful and perhaps even within our reach?

Today discipline by parents and teachers is sometimes represented as cruelty. Many children are being taught to take, seldom to give. When they become adolescents they expect the process to continue. They give nothing but keep on looking for more. And, when they fail to get more, their lack of discipline causes them to strike out in vandalism, hooliganism and even rioting. In these circumstances the cult of the anti-hero comes into its own.

It seems to me that stories about heroes and heroines are necessary to sweeten the sour flavour that has become evident in real life: stories which prove that even without discos, skateboard parks, community halls, music centres, television and trampolines, without organized games or parties of any kind, boys and girls can still become happy and fulfilled men and women.

I believe that we, the older generation, are failing our children. We are failing to provide them with an ideal. And with the knowledge that the power behind a nuclear mushroom cloud is the same as that behind the opening petals of a rose.

Index

was Mrs Belle Robertson, a farmer's daughter from Southend. She is trim, athletic, feminine, with a world-wide reputation as a gallant sportswoman. Had she been born sixty years earlier, all her gallantry might have been dissipated in a blur of milking, churning and cheese-making, and this male member of her home club in Southend might never have been able to remark, proudly, 'I have played golf with Belle at Dunaverty ever since she was a little girl.'

Many of the farmers in Southend used to keep their money in a sideboard drawer in the 'good room'. Today they employ the banks to execute financial deals more readily associated with city tycoons. But few of them are interested in accountancy, which has become as important a factor in farming as in every other trade and profession. (Including authorship, I may add, in a sour aside.) But like their fathers and grandfathers, who left difficult, finicky jobs like milking, churning and cheese-making to their wives and daughters, many of them now leave them to cope instead with the hard grind of paperwork.

In the drab days, however, there were farmers who did their best to lighten the work of their ladies.

I was often sent by my mother to collect butter and eggs from Dalmore, about a mile away along the riverside from the Manse. The tenant of this farm was nick-named Owld Yadi. Lean and loud-voiced, even at the age of sixty he presented a patriarchal appearance. His grey beard was long and straggly. His eyes, deep sunk in hollow cheeks, seemed to flash fire. He looked like the prophet Abraham pictured in the big family Bible at the Manse (in which all our birth dates were recorded); but in spite of such a holy association I was scared of him. When I encountered him in the fields or in the farmyard I walked warily, giving him a wide berth as I sought the safety of the kitchen and a warm welcome from his wife and daughter. (I was accustomed to carrying out similar manoeuvres if confronted by his Ayrshire bull.)

One day, approaching Dalmore, I was crossing the apparently deserted farmyard when a roar occurred behind me and Owld Yadi emerged from the barn, waving a knobbly walking stick in my direction: a stick which seemed to

threaten dreadful pain and sorrow. Indeed, he looked so dangerous that I took to my heels and made for the fence separating the yard from the open fields beyond.

'Stop! Stop!' he bellowed.

I flung myself at the fence and had almost thrust my way through when the seat of my trousers was caught in the barbed wire. It was like a nightmare. The pounding feet came closer. I could imagine the stick raised high to add to the pain in my bottom.

'Whit are ye daein', ye stupid wee bugger?' The voice crackled like thunder.

I waited for the blows. None came. Instead, I felt his hands on my trousers, extricating me from the wire.

Roughly he clutched my arm and hauled me upright. 'Whit's wrang wi' ye? I was only gaun tae ask if ye wanted a sweetie.'

The relief was so great that I could say nothing. He took a peppermint from his pocket. It was covered with fluff and traces of glaur.

'There ye are noo. Away inside an' the wife'll gi'e ye a piece.'

Still shaking, I took the sweetie and did what I was told. It was revealed to me then what a trapped bird must feel when liberated from a garden net by a loud, enormous human being.

Owld Yadi had surprised me by betraying a glint of kindness behind a grey exterior. He surprised other farmers – and his own family – by his invention and building of a machine for stirring the cheese vat.

In the yard, just outside the dairy, he erected a stout wooden pole, some forty feet high. Through a pulley at the top he threaded a thin wire rope, with a heavy metal weight attached. At the bottom end the rope was wound round a metal shaft. This was connected, through a hole in the wall, with an intricate system of gear wheels inside the dairy. Those wheels operated a flail-like arm which, at speed, accomplished the heavy task of stirring the curd in the cheese vat.

The apparatus worked on the principle of a grandfather

*On the following pages are details of Arrow
books that will be of interest.*

ROCKS IN MY SCOTCH

Angus MacVicar

A fascinating and affectionate account of the author's boyhood and life in his beloved Mull of Kintyre where his father – the redoubtable Padre – was minister for forty-seven years. The vista widens, too, to Scotland as a whole to make a joyful mixture of anecdote, history, legend and reminiscence which is rich with the writer's love of his land and his people.

Angus MacVicar's stories range from the dramatic and tragic to the humorous and hilarious – and sometimes he is even a little annoyed with the modern world – but always they are a delight to read – again and again.

'Delightful' *Sunday Express*

ABOUT MY FATHER'S BUSINESS

Lillian Beckwith

Lillian Beckwith already has an enormous following for her books about life on a Hebridean island.

Now she takes us back to her childhood, to the years before the Second World War, when her father ran a small grocer's shop in a Cheshire town.

It was typical of so many corner shops – the shops that are now more and more becoming just a memory, overwhelmed by redevelopment and the march of the supermarket. The corner shop where customers were known, often friends, not just faces at a check-out point, where shopping was gossipy and un-hurried.

A shop that is brought to life by the acute, affectionate memories of the little girl who grew up in it.

THE HILLS IS LONELY

Lillian Beckwith

When Lillian Beckwith advertised for a quiet, secluded place in the country, she received the following unorthodox description of the attractions of life on an isolated Hebridean croft:

'Surely it's that quiet here even the sheeps themselves on the hills is lonely and as to the sea it's that near I use it myself every day for the refusals . . .'

Intrigued by her would-be landlady's letter and spurred on by the sceptism of her friends, Lillian Beckwith replied in the affirmative. THE HILLS IS LONELY is the hilarious and enchanting story of the extremely unusual rest cure that followed.

A BORDER BAIRN

Lavinia Derwent

'I can see it all as plainly as if I were there in the farmhouse kitchen in the Cheviots, sitting on the rug in the lamplight with the big black kettle spitting and the sheep dip calendar hanging on the wall.'

And Lavinia Derwent evokes all that magic for us, too, in her enchanting childhood world of wide-eyed innocence and country wisdom, where Jessie, Jock-the-herd and Auld Baldy-Heid still rule unchallenged and dreams come true.

In this successor to the much-loved *A Breath of Border Air* and *Another Breath of Border Air*, the border bairn feels her first growing pains as she starts grammar school, has her first holiday away from home, and meets The Ragamuffin. This is a book for all who love the gentle humour and tranquillity of true country life.

'A gentle, lyrical evocation' *Oxford Mail*

'The best of Lavinia Derwent's books about her country life' *Glasgow Evening Times*

A BREATH OF BORDER AIR

Lavinia Derwent

'Looking back, I often wonder if any of it was real . . .'

Lavinia Derwent, well known as a best-selling author of children's books and as a television personality, here memorably portrays a childhood spent on a lonely farm in the Scottish Border country.

Here was an enchanted world of adventure: a world of wayward but endearing farm animals, and of local characters like Jock-the-herd . . . and Lavinia's closest friend, Jessie, who never failed to temper her earthy wisdom with a rare sense of humour.

'Any exiled Scot will breathe this fine air with joy' *Yorkshire Post*

ONE SMALL FOOTPRINT

Molly Weir

In her newest book, Molly Weir describes a life filled to the brim with hectic activities both inside and outside the Lyons' den. Ordinary things, like learning to drive a car or sending a telegram to the BBC, have some unusual results, and the not-so-ordinary – like the Lyons' transfer to television – often give rise to new hilarity.

As with her previous bestselling books, *One Small Footprint* is rich and overflowing with warmth, humour and the irrepressible Molly Weir's delight in people and in life. All who have enjoyed following her adventures from the tenements of Glasgow to the Lyons' den will be equally delighted by this, her sixth sparkling book of anecdotes and reminiscences. Once again, Molly proves how fully she lives up to her own maxim: 'Today is the first day of the rest of your life. Don't waste it.'

TRAVELS WITH FORTUNE

Christina Dodwell

Christina Dodwell has shared meals with cannibals, been treated by witch doctors, and been arrested as a spy. She has paddled one thousand miles down the Congo in a native dugout and hitchhiked rides on everything from an ancient lorry to a plane.

It all began when she found herself stranded in Africa, without money or transport. What had begun as a rather ordinary overland holiday became a three-year voyage of adventure and discovery through an Africa few visitors ever see. This is the story of that remarkable journey and the story of a rich and fascinating continent, as seen through the eyes of an English girl travelling alone.

'One of the best travel adventure books I have read for a long time' *Chris Bonington*
'An amazing and heartwarming story' *Country Life*

BESTSELLING SCOTTISH BOOKS
FROM ARROW

All these books are available from your bookshop or news-agent or you can order them direct. Just tick the titles you want and complete the form below.

☐	A CROFT IN CLACHAN	Sybil Armstrong	85p
☐	A BORDER BAIRN	Lavinia Derwent	85p
☐	A BREATH OF BORDER AIR	Lavinia Derwent	£1.25
☐	GOD BLESS THE BORDERS	Lavinia Derwent	£1.25
☐	ONE SMALL FOOTPRINT	Molly Weir	£1.25
☐	WALKING INTO THE LYONS' DEN	Molly Weir	85p
☐	ROCKS IN MY SCOTCH	Angus MacVicar	£1.25
☐	BEES IN MY BONNET	Angus MacVicar	£1.75
☐	BRUACH BLEND	Lillian Beckwith	£1.60
☐	BEAUTIFUL JUST	Lillian Beckwith	£1.60
☐	LIGHTLY POACHED	Lillian Beckwith	£1.60
☐	GREEN HAND	Lillian Beckwith	£1.60
☐	THE HILLS IS LONELY	Lillian Beckwith	£1.60
☐	A ROPE – IN CASE	Lillian Beckwith	£1.60
☐	THE SEA FOR BREAKFAST	Lillian Beckwith	£1.60

Postage _____

Total _____

ARROW BOOKS, BOOKSERVICE BY POST, PO BOX 29, DOUGLAS, ISLE OF MAN, BRITISH ISLES

Please enclose a cheque or postal order made out to Arrow Books Limited for the amount due including 15p per book for postage and packing for orders both within the UK and overseas.

Please print clearly

NAME ....

ADDRESS ....

....

Whilst every effort is made to keep prices down and to keep popular books in print, Arrow Books cannot guarantee that prices will be the same as those advertised here or that the books will be available.

BESTSELLING BIOGRAPHIES
FROM ARROW

All these books are available from your bookshop or news-
agent or you can order them direct. Just tick the titles you
require and complete the form below.

☐	IN THE BELLY OF THE BEAST	Jack Henry Abbott	£1.50
☐	THANKS TO RUGBY	Bill Beaumont	£1.95
☐	EVERYWHERE FOR WALES	Phil Bennett	£1.50
☐	TWO-WHEEL TREK	Neil Clough	£1.75
☐	TRAVELS WITH FORTUNE	Christina Dodwell	£1.50
☐	KIRI	David Fingleton	£2.50
☐	ONE STEP AT A TIME	Marie Joseph	£1.60
☐	MCVICAR BY HIMSELF	John McVicar	£1.60

Postage _____

Total _____

**ARROW BOOKS, BOOKSERVICE BY POST, PO BOX 29,
DOUGLAS, ISLE OF MAN, BRITISH ISLES**

Please enclose a cheque or postal order made out to Arrow Books
Limited for the amount due including 15p per book for postage and
packing for orders both within the UK and overseas.

Please print clearly

NAME ....

ADDRESS ....

....

Whilst every effort is made to keep prices down and to keep popular
books in print, Arrow Books cannot guarantee that prices will be the
same as those advertised here or that the books will be available.